Portraits of Rome

Volume 1

GIOVANNA NAPPI
&
MARELLA MALANDRINO

Second Edition 2025

To our dearest daughters, Tanya and Francesca, who encouraged our curiosity in exploring Rome, showing great passion and commitment.

&

To all curious readers who want to get lost in Rome.

Acknowledgements

We would like to thank our precious guide and art historian, Egidia Coda, for her valuable artistic support and revision. We also want to be grateful to our friend and art historian Marina Marinelli for her suggestions and encouragement. It's our pleasure to remember all the guides who accompanied us in exploring the city and fostering our curiosity.

We would like to thank all those we met on the spot and who enhanced our explorations of churches, courtyards, palaces and interesting sites with anecdotes, curiosities and personal experiences.

Our gratitude goes to our husbands, Vittorio and Giovanni, who gave us continuous and supportive feedback on our work.

We thank the photographer Mariangela Caturano for her contribution to the book cover.

About the Authors

Giovanna and Marella's friendship and collaboration dates back to the time when they were both English language and literature colleagues in a high school in Rome and had the opportunity to develop international projects that involved many people, especially young people, in dynamic, lively and productive contexts both in Italy and abroad.

Their belief is that travelling is a crucial element in individual cultural growth, greatly contributing to broadening one's horizons towards different realities. In this spirit, therefore, they set out on an exploratory 'journey' of their city, recording their emotions, impressions and sensations being prompted by the places they had already known for a long time but never observed deeply—somewhat like taking a step back for a closer look.

This book is the sum of their efforts together.

CONTENTS

INTRODUCTION

"I may not attempt to report in its fulness our young woman's response to the deep appeal of Rome, to analyse her feelings as she trod the pavement of the Forum or to number her pulsations as she crossed the threshold of Saint Peter's... she had always been fond of history, and here was history in the stones of the street and the atoms of the sunshine. She had an imagination that kindled at the mention of great deeds, and wherever she turned some great deed had been acted. These things strongly moved her, but moved her all inwardly...... Rome confessed to the psychological moment. The herd of reechoing tourists had departed, and most of the solemn places had relapsed into solemnity. The sky was a blaze of blue, and the plash of the fountains in their mossy niches had lost its chill and doubled its music. On the corners of the warm, bright streets, one stumbled on bundles of flowers." (Henry James "The Portrait of a Lady"1881)

The description that Henry James offers of a 19th century Rome in his novel "The Portrait of a Lady", perfectly captures the atmosphere and the emotional explosion that is released in front of such a beauty. Walking through its streets, alleys, lanes and squares in search of its incomparable treasures arouses a feeling of wonder and prompts curiosity to explore pieces of evidence of the past that has been stratified in deeply different times. The most attractive aspect is its variety, often concentrated in a single image, which nevertheless combines elements from different worlds, cultures and peoples.

Walking and treading that ground that in the past has seen wealthy Roman patricians, servants, consuls, emperors and later knights, ladies and feudal lords, as well as the great artists of the Renaissance such as Michelangelo, Raphael and Bramante, can easily be a cue inspiring an ideal film set for successful movies. These places have been creating a sense of renewed wonder that accompanies anyone who is about to discover its secrets. What about distinguished figures like Bernini and Borromini, who have undoubtedly contributed to improving the face of the city with their impressive works?

But what really catches the viewer, traps his soul and awakens his curiosity are the continuous steps through different moments of history, shown by the ruins of the imperial era, the medieval squares, the impressive Renaissance palaces, as well as monuments and churches that enshrine all their signs. These layers allow us to find evidence of the past even on a single site such as the Basilica of San Clemente, whose basement still keeps the remains of the god Mithras' worship and where we can still admire the oldest inscription in vernacular Italian painted on a wall and finally discover a cosmatesque floor and frescoes where even Masaccio's hand can be noticed.

View of Fori

Walking through these places becomes for each of us a unique opportunity to live history again, almost as protagonists, sharing the same emotions, passions and experiences as those lived by our ancestors.

Sometimes, you happen to meet common people along your way, guardians of churches and doorkeepers of ancient buildings, who spontaneously offer their knowledge acquired over the years in the form of facts that really existed, legends that have been passed down, and funny tales. They are the ones who watch over the great works of art and, by winking, offer their secrets to anyone who wants to learn more.

Rome is so rich in art that some sites are not always accessible, namely the so-called Gladiator's Tomb, whose recent discovery has amazed many people. In 2008, along Via Flaminia, a 7-meter-deep stretch of an ancient consular road was discovered. Along with it, a beautifully preserved monumental complex contains the remains of a mausoleum belonging to a Roman general leader of Marcus Aurelius' army. The general's deeds had affinities with those of the famous character in the movie "The Gladiator" by Ridley Scott, therefore, it was named the Gladiator's Tomb. Further excavations carried out on the site brought to light an authentic military necropolis dating back to the time of Emperor Constantine, a group of praetorian steles and a *fullonica*, a workshop for the washing and dyeing of soldiers' clothes.

It is so exciting to propose walks that trace the marks of overlapping and show their magnetic force that drags you back in time throughout the complexity and variety of history. The sequence of historical periods is not the only characteristic of the city; even the sudden appearance of an ancient ruin that we would never imagine to be there can be amazing. An example of this can be found in Augusto Imperatore Square, where the presence of the impressive mausoleum, begun in the first century B.C., fits into a context of much more modern streets and buildings, such as the latest restoration of *Ara Pacis*, a museum dedicated to victorious military campaigns of the Emperor Augustus and recently restored by Richard Myer. This gives the place a unique and extraordinary dimension. A walk in Piazza Campo de' Fiori could be just as surprising, when among the swarm of people walking and stopping under the statue of Giordano Bruno, and half raising your eyes, you can see the coats of arms of two popes who left important traces in the political and artistic events of Renaissance: Alessandro VI

Borgia and Giulio II della Rovere, notable historical figures and creators of impressive artistic achievements.

Just a few more metres towards Piazza Navona, we will suddenly find ourselves in front of the statue of Pasquino, a Hellenistic statue from the 3rd century B.C., to which the Roman people have always entrusted their complaints against the power, as was the case with three other 'talking' statues in Rome. It was accidentally confined to a corner of the homonymous little square because Cardinal Carafa (1517-1561), a wealthy and influential landowner in the neighbourhood, considered it unworthy of the collection of fine statues in his palace and decided to get rid of it. When Pope Leo XII, the unpopular Pope della Genga, died, an irreverent epitaph was left on the statue: "Here della Genga lies, for his and our peace". Moreover, the ominous Pope died during the Carnival period, thus interrupting the only time of the year in which joyful celebrations were allowed in the streets, and Pasquino had the opportunity to say: "Three spites did you do us, O Holy Father, accept the papacy, live so long, die on Carnival to be mourned".

Roman people are by nature humorous and irreverent, and therefore, they like mocking important and unpopular people by using satires and humorous words. During the papacy of Leo XII, Giuseppe Gioacchino Belli, a Roman poet, was in full literary activity; perhaps he knew something about those mocking invectives!

In this book, you will find impressionistic descriptions of the most popular *rioni* and areas of Rome, which include some art, history, anecdotes, and quotations mixed with personal feelings and emotions released whenever hidden corners and unexplored treasures are discovered and this is what makes this city an inexhaustible source of wonder.

ESQUILINO AND MONTI

Monti Lane

A visit to the city often begins in the Monti neighbourhood, whose name comes from the many ups and downs that characterise most of its streets. It is located in the very heart of the city, not far from the Colosseum, the Imperial Forum and the Basilica of Santa Maria Maggiore. The beating heart of ancient Rome can be identified with the Imperial Forums, a series of five monumental squares built between 46 B.C. and 113 A.D. by the city's greatest emperors, Caesar, Augustus, Vespasian, Nerva and Trajan. They were in line with the growing expansion of the Empire and the need for larger public buildings as well as the desire to make the emperors' great achievements more visible.

Rione Monti takes up a large part of the area that was known as the Suburra in ancient Rome. That area was inhabited by the urban lower class who lived in poor conditions, and the term 'suburra' refers to particularly degraded areas still today. It would draw its name from 'sub urbe', hence the term 'suburb'. This confirms the fact that since Roman times, the wealthy have lived in the upper areas, whereas the poor have lived in the lower ones.

"To the atrocious libido

Every street was Suburra."

Even Gabriele d'Annunzio had used the word 'Suburra' in its literary meaning of ill-famed neighbourhood; it was the area of the city corresponding to the present neighbourhood Monti, close to the Imperial Forums. Among its narrow, noisy and dirty alleys, since the third century B.C., the daily life of the most popular Rome had taken place, the one of the actors, gladiators and courtesans. 'Suburra' was the most dangerous place: a refuge for prostitutes, thieves and outlaws. After sunset, those who dared to walk in its streets challenged their destiny and used to do it accompanied by armed slaves with torches. For security reasons and for the continuous fires, the rich patricians in power had a wall built around the neighbourhood, thus highlighting the social difference between the rich Rome and the Suburra. The wall, made of peperino blocks, gabine stone and travertine, up to 33 metres high, was built under Emperor Augustus to isolate and protect the forum. Like all popular places, also Suburra had its celebrities: Julius Caesar (100 B.C. - 44 B.C.) and the poet Martial (40 A.D. to 104 A.D.) were born there.

Suburra was in the heart of another Rome, the Rome of taverns and brothels, also tolerated by the powerful and the rich people who used to go there to satisfy their lust. According to the biographers Suetonius and Tacitus, even Valeria Messalina (25 A.D. - 48 A.D.), the wife of Emperor Claudius, used to disguise herself as a prostitute, wearing a red wig and went to the neighbourhood, where she repeatedly indulged herself. During her secret wanderings, she used Lysisca as a fictitious name meaning 'bitch woman' and went to brothels with heavy make-up to offer herself to sailors and gladiators. Nero as well used to disguise himself as a poor man to get the people's rumours about his government and to test the mood of the people about his ruling. Suburra was also the site of the Carinae area, located on an originally residential and aristocratic hilltop, which owes its name to the particular shape of the ground, with two large rocks in the form of 'carinae', i.e. hulls of ships. In the mid-6th century B.C. the area was included by Servius Tullius among the four city regions. Palatina, Collina, Suburana and Esquilina. The neighbourhood was crossed by the Argileto, an ancient Roman street of the I century A.D., which connected the place to the Roman Forum (today's via Leonina and via della Madonna dei Monti).

Via Leonina

It is worth mentioning via In Selci, whose name derives from ancient 'silices' of Roman pavement found during restoration works in the area, perhaps traces of the old *Vicus Suburanus* where the road is located, bordering the neighbourhood and called *Caput Suburrae*. The street was also named 'In Orphea', because of a nymphaeum or a large fountain. During the Middle Ages, it was denominated "Clivo di San Martino" because it led to the basilica San Martino ai Monti on the homonymous square. Today it is called "In Selci" again because of the church built there in the Middle Ages. Aristocratic palaces and towers were built on the ruins of the Suburra and the Fori, some of which are still preserved, albeit modified, such as Torre dei Conti, Torre delle Milizie at Mercati Traianei, Torre dei Borgia in S. Pietro in Vincoli, Torre dei Capocci Arcioni and the Torre del Grillo. The 30-metre-high Torre dei Conti is located between Via Cavour, Largo Ricci and Via dei Fori Imperiali. It was completed by Riccardo Conti, Pope Innocent III's brother, and was named after Lotario dei Conti di Segni, who became Pope as Innocent III. It was built on the ruins of the "Templum Telluris", but due to an earthquake, it collapsed and was left as no more than a ruin until 1620. It was then rebuilt by the Apostolic Chamber and later by Pope Urban VIII.

Strolling through this area once again, we end up at Foro Traiano, where, in 107 A.D., the Emperor wanted to build the monumental complex that was certainly the most perfect of all. It worked at the same time as a forum, a temple, a basilica, a library, a market and it extended from the present loggia of the Rhodian knights to the whole palace of the Prefecture.

Emperor Traiano had the hill cut and created the modern terrace that is at the same level as Via Cesare Battisti, the complex extends for about 300 meters, and it is 200 meters wide, nearly covering six acres of land. Inside the structure, Traiano Column is a true live documentary about the conquest of Dacia, made up of a marble layer 200m long and winding around a shaft in a spiral. It contains 2500 figures sculpted in relief, and it actually represents the mausoleum of Traiano. On both sides of the column are located two libraries with books from Greek and Latin collections.

Torre dei Conti

Here is the Forum, which must have been a stunning construction, where two exedras were the backdrop, one towards the Capitol and the other towards the Quirinal Hill, which is still visible to anyone passing along the Via dei Fori. Almost all archaeologists agree in calling markets those small rooms on the ground and on the first floor, which were not used as retail shops, but were used as stores by the wholesalers who distributed the goods coming in from Magnanapoli. It seems that this was not the place where the merchants would come to sell but rather where the State toll contractors would sell wholesale products to the merchants. The vast hall on the upper floor was used as a commodity exchange hall, where the imperial officers noted down the items in demand and offered those available at the time. There were also rooms for storage and numerous workshops where retailers could buy any unsold goods.

Mercati Traianei

In the 13th century, this area became the theatre of controversy between important noble families, such as the Caetani and the Colonna, who contended some areas between Magnanapoli and the Traiano Column. Evidence of this dispute was the majestic Tower of the Militia, built by the Caetani family, where the Emperor from the Sacred Roman Empire Arrigo VII, was hosted at the beginning of the 14th century to be protected from the popular fury stirred up by a member of the Colonna family. It is perhaps the tallest tower in the city, rising up 50 metres like a modern skyscraper as if to control the entire area and remind later generations of the splendour and power of the past. Until the 19th century, this place was also the setting for other sorts of disputes between youngsters who used to fight against each other, the "Monticiani" and the "Trasteverini", to win the title of the oldest neighbourhood of Rome by means of... blows of rocks, still remembered as 'sassaiole'.

At the end of the 19th century, the Monti neighbourhood was heavily remodelled with the opening of Via Cavour and Via degli Annibaldi. It was then characterized by buildings constructed in the typical *Umbertine* style, imported to Rome by the Piemontese officials of the Ministry of National Works, a style not very much in tune with the features of the small streets where some ancient noble palaces were still dominating. One of the most typical streets is via Baccina, which was an aristocratic road in the 17th century and where you can still see portals in grey stone or marble, grafted onto buildings rebuilt in 1700 but certainly belonging to pre-existing buildings of the 15th and 16th centuries.

The church of S. Maria ai Monti is located where a convent of Clarisse nuns once stood and which was later converted into dwelling houses with barns. It is said that towards the end of the

1500s, some workers, while demolishing a wall of the barn, heard a voice begging them not to hurt the child. The astonished workers removed the bricks with their hands and found a beautiful fresco representing the Virgin with the Child. The news was spread, attracting a large number of pilgrims and the site became such a miraculous place that Pope Gregory XIII decided to have a church built there. It is a fine example of late Mannerist art and contains works by Cesare Nebbia, Durante Alberti, Girolamo Muziano and Giacomo della Porta. On the street you will also find many craft stores, typical small shops and taverns, confirming the very old Roman tradition of eating and drinking in good company.

The Fori

Via Urbana

Typical buildings in Monti

As we move on to explore the neighbourhood, we enter a maze of narrow streets, alleyways and small squares where the sound of the water, flowing from the fountains scattered around, keeps you company, especially at sunset, when the high-pitched chatter that floods the narrow streets slowly fades away. It is a delightful friend, especially in the summer when the dry air that envelops the body and parches the throat is gently eased by the relieving sips of the freshwater flowing abundantly from the springs.

Monti Fountain

Thus you end up in Via degli Zingari, which takes its name from the many gypsy caravans that have flocked to Rome since the 17th century. The men used to shape metal pots and dishes, while the women went telling fortune to passers-by for money in return. A plaque reminding of the Nazi-Fascist genocide of the Nomads and the Jews can be seen there. The area was originally called Pozzo di Proba, perhaps either because of the presence of a well or due to the close Via del Pozzuolo. On the street, you can admire sacred shrines dedicated to the Virgin Mary, also called "Madonnelle", often placed on the buildings' corners.

"Madonnelle"

In the 16th and 17th centuries, Via dei Serpenti was considered the main street of the Monti neighbourhood, and its name seems to be related to various theories: one refers to the snake-infested countryside, the second associates its name to a family called

Serpenti, the third connects its name to an image of the Virgin Mary crushing a snake, and the fourth is linked to an image of Laocoonte surrounded by snakes. The street was originally much longer and went around the church of S. Lorenzo in Panisperna, the site of San Lorenzo's martyrdom. Here, according to a medieval tradition, the friars used to offer bread and ham (panis et perna) to the poor, hence the name of Via Panisperna, a place rich in historical memories, including the life of St. Brigid, who gave her name to the Brigidine Sisterhood. Walking onwards to Magnanapoli and lingering to look back behind, an image of a roller-coaster-like road appears, edging at the top with the huge dome of Santa Maria Maggiore Basilica. It is one of the two city roads that cross several hills: it goes down from the Quirinale, climbs up the Viminale and comes down to rise up again to the Esquilino. Via Panisperna immediately evokes memories of the group of scientists who passed into history thanks to their passion for scientific research. It was in the Institute of Physics, located on this street, that the seven young scientists lived and shared moments of enthusiasm and scientific glory, carrying out cutting-edge research into the atomic nucleus and artificial radioactivity. Echoes of this intellectual energy, reinforced by the leading power of young scientists, spread beyond the national borders despite the well-known difficulties that characterised the years leading up to the Second World War. This historical moment in our past was beautifully narrated by Gianni Amelio in his 1989 movie 'I ragazzi di via Panisperna'.

Once on top of the road in the direction of Via Nazionale and leaving Villa Aldombrandini, a true jewel of Renaissance architecture, on your right, you will get to Largo Magnanapoli, and there you have to make a choice: which direction to take, up towards the Quirinale or down towards the Fori along the Salita del Grillo? The second option will lead you back to the Monti neighbourhood, where you can see the residence of the Marchese del Grillo and the homonymous tower, just a few steps away. Passing by the large Palazzo Veniero on the left, built on the ruins of the ancient church "S.Salvatore de Militis", we cross the arch and end up in the delightful Piazzetta del Grillo where at number 5, the magnificent baroque portal of the palace stands out. The building immediately evokes the famous character so well played by Alberto Sordi in Mario Monicelli's popular movie 'Il marchese del Grillo', a beloved semi-fictional character. What we do know for sure is that he might have been rich, well-to-do and enjoyed mocking the Roman aristocracy, especially the powerful, the proud and those who were granted special privileges. He must have belonged to one of the two Del Grillo families who lived between the seventeenth and nineteenth centuries. Over time, the eighteenth-century palace has belonged to various noble families who have always kept the frescoed interiors and looked after the nymphos in the large garden. At the beginning of the 20th century, the famous painter Renato Guttuso added prestige to the palace as the artist bought some of the rooms to make his own studio and home.

The above-mentioned phenomenon of stratification gives the city and in particular the Monti neighbourhood, a unique identity, like the speaking voice that gives soul and character to the place. It is no coincidence that this venue, as well as being the background for popular legends, local traditions, folklore and ancient myths, has also often been used as a setting for many famous movies from the post-war years to the present day. Indeed, this 'rione' has always attracted both artists and celebrities, and it is just while strolling along Via dei Serpenti that looking up at number 29, you will see a plaque on the façade dedicated to Mario Monicelli with the following words: "Here lived Mario Monicelli, master of cinema and free man, 1915-2010".

The popular heart of the Monti neighbourhood, where Piazza Suburra still exists, has resisted over the centuries, throughout the Middle Ages and the Renaissance, until the restyling of Rome at the end of the 19th century, after the Porta Pia Breach. In 1870, when the Piemontese entered Rome, and the city became the capital of the new Italian State, many urban changes took place in the area of Monti, both with the construction of large buildings and with the opening of a road directly connecting to Termini railway station. In that period, the City Council decided to assign new names to many streets in the zone and to dedicate one of them to Cavour, Prime Minister of the Sardinian Reign. But it was only in 1886 that the works for this new stretch of Via Cavour started.

After popes, invaders, and architects had completed their work, *gentrification* was the process that transformed the old Roman suburbs into trendy places, thanks to their central position. Monti has many faces: during the day, it is a cheerful and busy neighbourhood that mainly lives on tourism, and where it is pleasant to walk aimlessly, whereas, at night, it becomes the reign of the wildest nightlife, almost reliving the atmosphere of its ancient origin. Starting from Piazza della Suburra, we walk along Via Urbana (ancient Vicus Patricius), which includes some of the most beautiful buildings of the entire area, preserving its exclusive elegance, as well as the charm of the stores, the originality of the many shrines dedicated to the Madonna and her Child Jesus. Among the various buildings to be remembered is the ancient Manzoni theatre, where the great actor Ettore Petrolini, also born in Monti, lived in Via Baccina in the early years of the 20th century. Some of these noble palaces are linked to very old stories and legends, among which the most peculiar and perhaps the bloodiest one concerns King Servio Tullio during the ancient Roman monarchy, the one who had promoted the moving of patrician homes into this area.

From Via Urbana, taking Via Leonina, you will get to the so-called Salita dei Borgia that leads up to the Basilica of S. Pietro in Vincoli. The staircase, also known as "Vicus Scelleratus," is related to stories of violent events that have occurred over the centuries and date back to Roman times. According to Tito Livio, in 535 B.C., the youngest daughter of King Servio Tullio, Tullia Minor, an ambitious and cunning woman, fell in love and was returned by her brother-in-law Tarquinio, and together devised a criminal plan to get rid of their mutual partners and crown their 'love'. They ordered to have them murdered, and once married, they had their elderly father, Servio Tullio, killed so that the kingdom could freely pass into the hands of the greedy husband, Tarquinio. What made the murder of Servio Tullio more ferocious was the way in which his daughter Tullia, at the sight of her father dying on the ground, ran him over with her chariot without any scruple or remorse.

In the early 15th century, the name Borgia was given to the staircase in relation to the residence of Vannozza Cattanei, a woman remembered for being the official lover of Cardinal Rodrigo Borgia, who was elected as Pope Alexander VI in 1492 and by whom she had four children. She was the mother of two famous historical characters, Cesare and Lucrezia Borgia and had lived in Rome for a long time, managing one of the city's most famous and popular inns, carrying out activities of dubious morality. Traces of her life can be found in the building that dominates the staircase. The façade is more graceful thanks to a balcony adorned with friezes and also linked to the traditional legend, according to which Vannozza and her daughter Lucrezia were used to lean out, attracting passers-by with their beauty. In the 19th century, whenever Lord Byron walked there, he fancied seeing Lucrezia on the balcony and was so attracted to her that he wanted to get hold of a lock of her blond hair.

Salita dei Borgia

The uphill slope is not too steep and is easy to climb, especially if you imagine what this place must have looked like in the days of ancient Rome. On top of the staircase, after crossing the narrow dark tunnel, we find ourselves in S. Pietro in Vincoli square, dominated by the homonymous basilica, whose meaning 'vincoli' is linked to the chains of St.Peter's imprisonment in Rome and that was built between 422 and 470 A.D. to commemorate a miracle which took place there. The tradition of the church tells how the chains that had belonged to St. Peter were found during a journey to Palestine and then given to the mother of the founder of this church, Eudossia. A miraculous event is linked to the narration of this episode: when the pope compared the chains coming from Jerusalem to those that had been lying in the Mamertine Prison for a long time, he noticed how they merged almost miraculously. Thus, the Basilica is strictly linked to the miracle of the fusion as evidence of the strong bond between the Eastern and Western Empires and perhaps of an ideal will to unify the two religious realities. The urn of St. Peter's Chains completed in 1856, is kept in a reliquary with two statues on either side representing St. Peter and the Liberating Angel in the centre of the marble altar. The chains are composed of two pieces, those of the Roman prison, formed by twenty-three rings plus a collar and those of Jerusalem, with eleven smaller rings. Undoubtedly, the period of greatest splendour of the Basilica was the Renaissance, thanks to the restoration work promoted by Pope Giulio II that included the entrance portico, the adjoining convent and the cloister attributed to Giuliano da Sangallo. His tomb had to be built in this basilica for his will, having commissioned the works to Michelangelo in 1505. But the grandeur of the project, which foresaw the realization of a mausoleum with more than forty statues, involved works that, subjected to continuous variations, were concluded 35 years after the death of the Pope himself. The last version of the project included only seven statues, among which the famous Moses by Michelangelo which towers at the centre of the mausoleum, is considered one of the most harmonious sculptural works of the Renaissance. The sarcophagus that was to contain the body of

Giulio II, preserved today in St. Peter's Basilica, is positioned above Moses, and a statue representing the Pope lying on his side is placed on its lid.

Then we return to Via Urbana as far as the site of the so-called "Titulus Pudentis", built in the 2nd century A.D., the home of the Roman senator Pudente, famous for being a Christian martyr, together with his daughters Pudenziana and Prassede, and for frequently hosting St. Peter in his home. In this place, Christianity wanted to leave its mark with the presence of churches built on pre-existing Roman private dwellings that, with the rise of Christianity, favoured by Emperor Constantine in the 4th century A.D., took the name of "domus ecclesiae" or "titulus". They were mainly located inside patrician houses and were converted into places of prayer, taking the name of their owner. They represented an important moment in the history of pastoral care, being at the origin of what would later become the parish. At the beginning of the fourth century, there were about 25 'tituli', including the basilicas of Santa Prassede, Santa Pudenziana and San Martino ai Monti. The area around the Basilica of Santa Pudenziana is rich in Roman remains, partly underground and partly embedded in the building, and recent excavations have revealed the presence of a two-storey house on top of which a thermal building was constructed in the 3rd century, whose original floor is unique and consists of fragments of amphorae arranged in a herringbone pattern. At the end of the 4th century, on the Pope's will, it was transformed into the present church. On the left of the façade stands the beautiful five-tier bell tower, dating back to the beginning of the 13th century. The façade, with the entablature of the central portal, is one of the most beautiful medieval reliefs in Rome, with a floral frieze and clypeus in which the figures of the Agnus Dei and the Saints Prassede, Pastore, Pudenziana and

Pudente are inscribed, dated around 1080. The restoration works carried out in 1588 turned the church into a single nave, building chapels in the aisles and thus revealing the ancient columns. In 1930, following the restoration works, the walls and the floor were removed and traces of the original walls of the thermal hall were found, as well as its mosaic floor. In the right aisle there is a fresco by Domenichino representing The Conversion of St. William of Aquitaine of 1625. Domenichino himself had stayed in the neighbouring Via S. Martino ai Monti at number 20, where the singular inscription dating to 1872 is located: "Domenico Zampieri Bolognese, called Domenichino, the glory of painting, in this house sheltered from the implacable war of envy". Indeed, his genius and creativity, but above all, his admirable artistic trait, are evident in his paintings, even though the beauty he sought in all its forms could not always make up for some dark sides of his character, which were dominated by obsessions of envy and meanness. Continuing to explore the interior of the church, you will notice that the apse still preserves the magnificent mosaic of the late 4th century, depicting Christ on the Throne, surrounded by the apostles and the Saints Pudenziana and Prassede, in the background Jerusalem and on top of it the symbols of the Evangelists. In the left aisle there is the Caetani Chapel, which rises on the site of the Saint Pastore's oratory, considered the first place of worship established in Pudente's house. The late 16th-century chapel, begun by Francesco da Volterra and finished by Carlo Maderno, is rich in marble, stuccoes, mosaics, and funerary monuments, among which stands out the one dedicated to Cardinal Luciano Bonaparte, Napoleon's nephew.

Basilica of Santa Pudenziana

Walking up Via Cavour to Piazzale dell'Esquilino, you will pass by the Basilica of Santa Maria Maggiore, which faces a majestic Corinthian marble column, 14 metres high, commissioned by Pope Paolo V Borghese (1605-1621) and made by Carlo Maderno. It is commonly known as the Column of Peace and is the only one remaining intact of the eight columns that supported the Basilica of Massenzio, known as the Temple of Peace in the Middle Ages. Looking up, following the vertical line of the monument and the superb façade of the basilica, you will be for a while pulled out of the noisy hustle and bustle of the large square with the many streets and alleys converging into that point.

Santa Maria Maggiore is one of the four papal basilicas in Rome along with San Giovanni in Laterano, San Pietro in Vaticano and San Paolo fuori le Mura. They enjoy the status of extraterritoriality established by the Lateran Pacts between the Italian State and the Holy See in 1929 and benefit from special advantages such as the papal altar and the Holy Door, which is opened by the Pope in a rite during the Holy Year. The wide front staircase suggests that since its origins (352-366), the church was erected on top of one of the Seven Hills, namely the Esquiline Hill, probably the highest point in Rome. It stands on top of the "Cispius," between the Rione Monti and the Esquiline. According to tradition, it was founded by Pope Liberius and then renovated during the papacy of Sisto III in the 5th century. Among the major Roman basilicas, it is the only one to have largely retained its original early Christian structure, although it has undergone several renovations in time, most recently with a new façade designed by Ferdinando Fuga in the 18th century. The bell tower is Romanesque style, built in the late 1300s, and is the tallest in Rome. Excavations around the middle of the last century brought to light a structure dating back to Roman times on which the basilica was later built. Some ancient mosaics by Filippo Rusuti can be seen on the façade. Its construction is said to be linked to a miraculous event: a snowfall on the fifth of August, an episode that is commemorated every year with solemn celebrations and a shower of white petals.

Santa Maria Maggiore

You enter quietly, almost frightened by the vastness and solemnity of the place. Light filters through the large stained-glass windows, radiating in multiple colours and illuminating the central nave. Inside the basilica is the Hall of the Popes, which forms a sort of Pantheon of famous people, such as cardinals, popes and members of the Spanish royal family. There is also a spiral staircase attributed to Gian Lorenzo Bernini connecting the five levels of the bishops' palace to the sacristy. Within the basilica, the remains of the two great architects, Pietro and Gianlorenzo Bernini, father and son, are preserved, with a plaque placed at the end of the right aisle.

Pietro and Gianlorenzo Bernini's tomb

Valadier's work transformed a pre-existing choir into the present baptistery, with a red porphyry basin surrounded by a marble balustrade. The centrepiece of the entire basilica building, commissioned by Pope Paul V, is the Pauline Chapel with 17th-century frescoes executed by Cavalier d'Arpino and decorations with precious and refined marbles to emphasize the originality of the tabernacle, designed by Giacomo Rainaldi, which contains the most important Marian sacred image, the Salus Populi Romani, attributed to St. Luca Evangelista, patron saint of all painters. It portrays the Madonna and Child on a cedar wooden panel. Tradition assigns the image a protective value against misfortune and disease, and the current Pope Francis visits the sacred image before every journey he takes and on his return as a form of thanksgiving. The Sforza Chapel, commissioned by the homonymous family, had the elder Michelangelo involved in the project, who devised an oblique rectangular plan, thus creating a movement. Worth visiting are the Cesi Chapel, the Chapel of the

Crucifix built by the architect Fuga, which is the most recent (Holy Year 1750), although it preserves a wooden Crucifix dating from the first half of the 15th century. At the same time, Ferdinando Fuga restored a Gothic chapel dedicated to St. Michael the Archangel. Another masterpiece that can be admired in the basilica is the Sacred Cradle by Virginio Vespignani, made in the mid-18th century and placed in front of the papal altar. It was crafted from different types of marble extracted from excavations in Rome and Ostia to remind us of the role of the church, which represented both the Western Bethlehem and the Nativity Basilica in Rome. The Sistine Chapel, also known as the Crib Chapel, was built in the late 1500s on the commission of Pope Sisto V and designed by the architect Domenico Fontana. Its structure has the shape of a Greek cross with two side chapels, and it is topped by large windows around the crib oratory, reproducing the cave of the Nativity in Bethlehem. Columns adorned with vine branches and porticoes recalling the appearance of Solomon's ancient temple represent another element related to the original worship of Jesus' birth. Besides the great works of art, two older and unique masterpieces stand out, representing the artist's desire to eternalize beauty throughout the centuries and convey a spiritual and symbolic message at the same time. Such is the case with the marble nativity scene created in 1291 by Arnolfo di Cambio.

The Nativity by Arnolfo di Cambio

It was the first crib known in art history and shows the nativity group with St. Joseph, Our Lady and the Child, the ox and the donkey flanked by the Magi, sculptured while approaching Our Lady to offer their gifts. The other ancient element that gives the basilica an original and unique appearance is the mosaics, divided into early Christian and medieval. The former are located on the nave and the Arch of Triumph illustrating the story of the Jewish people before and after the Tablets of the Law came into existence. They represent the evolution and development of Christianity. The mosaics of the Triumphal Arch, perfectly preserved, narrate the infancy of Jesus, while the medieval mosaics in the apse are attributed to Jacopo Torriti represent scenes from the life of Mary and the presentation of Jesus to the temple. In the upper part Mary is pictured in the moment of her coronation flanked by angels and saints. As you step out of the church into the porch, the Holy Door, a symbol of reconciliation with God and a new beginning, stands out in all its grandeur. It was made of bronze recently in the year 2000 and commemorates the Jubilees that have been held in Rome since 1300, initially every 50 years and then every 25 years. In the Jewish tradition, the Jubilee represented a year of resting for the land to make it more fertile, while in the Catholic tradition, it is the period when the pope grants plenary indulgence to the pilgrims who travel to Rome to attend religious rites. When the Holy Year begins, the four Holy Doors, St. Peter's, St. Mary Major, St. John Lateran and St. Paul Outside the Walls, are opened.

Continuing the walk near the square, we reach Via di Santa Prassede and the homonymous basilica, small and rather unremarkable, a precious jewel dating back to 817 and considered the richest example of medieval art in Rome, dedicated to the Holy Martyr. St. Prassede had a sad destiny like her sister Pudenziana and her father Pudentius; they were all martyred, and she is remembered for the episode in which, after collecting the blood of persecuted Christians with a sponge, had poured it into a well. The ancient 'titolo', which lies far below the present basilica and was originally the villa of Senator Pudente, was the first place where the Christians used to gather. It is dedicated to the saint and was transformed into the present church by Pope Pasquale I (817- 824), by annexing a convent of Greek rite and moving the relics of 2000 martyrs there from the catacombs; the church underwent several restorations, and after 1870 the convent was destroyed and replaced by a school. The main entrance, consisting of an important 12th-century prothyrum, was enclosed by the surrounding 18th-century buildings, making the devotees enter from the less crowded side street. The main façade was originally introduced by a portico and still retains the medieval frame. Inside, the Chapel of St. Zenone is considered the most important monument of Byzantine art in Rome.

It was commissioned by Pope Pasquale I as a mausoleum for his mother, Teodora and is accessible through a portal framed by two black marble columns supporting a cinerary urn with the remains of Zenone, the martyr priest. Once inside the chapel, the dazzling light from the vault, which is completely covered with Byzantine-style gold mosaics, is a delight to admire and, therefore, is also called "the Garden of Paradise". The symbolism of the scenic representation is extremely eloquent, depicting the images of Christ, the Virgin Mary, St.Prassede and Theodora. In a niche next to the chapel is the column of flagellation, a fragment brought from Jerusalem in 1223 and believed to be the one on which Jesus Christ was scourged. The cosmatesque floor, consisting of polychrome marbles of various shapes, dates back to a modern restoration, and a centrally positioned porphyry disc covers the well where St. Prassede is said to have shed the blood of the martyrs. Walking down the nave, we slowly approach an iconographic representation of great symbolic power which, with its brightly coloured mosaics inlaid with gold, tells us of a scene dominated by the figure of Christ surrounded by St Pudenziana and St Prassede, St. Peter and St. Paul embracing them, overlooked by a host of ancestors in the company of angels in a field of poppies. At the bottom of the scene, a frieze depicting grazing lambs borders the image. This masterpiece of Byzantine art, while confirming the canons of static art, conveys a deep emotional involvement, reinforcing the idea of a strong devotion achieved through sacrifice and martyrdom. Leaving the chapel, on the third pillar, stands the monument to Bishop G.B. Santoni, believed to be Bernini's first work made at the early age of only 16 (1614). On the opposite side, we find a remarkable chapel, built towards the end of the 16th century and commissioned by the Olgiati family, wealthy bankers from Como. The interior contains a series of works of art that are considered real masterpieces, in particular the frescoes by the famous Italian painter Giuseppe Cesari, better known as Cavalier D'Arpino. The two canvases at both sides of the altar depicting Sant'Andrea and San Bernardo di Chiaravalle were made by the above-mentioned artist. Precious ancient and medieval marble, as well as a beautiful thirteenth-century monument, contribute to making the interior of the basilica particularly rich and fascinating. From the presbytery, we have access to the crypt, also dating back to medieval time, of a semi-circular shape, where the relics of Saints Prassede and Pudenziana are kept in a sarcophagus. The 11th-century bell tower is hardly visible from the outside; it preserves some lively frescoes with martyrdom scenes. It is hard to leave this small church where you are enveloped in a deep silence, nestled in the scent of incense and where you are carried away by a mystical atmosphere and a strong taste of the past. The soft lighting the subdued, barely audible voices invite you to linger and stop to rejoice in the sense of peace and serenity.

St. Zenone's Chapel

Santa Prassede Basilica

As you leave the church, you are once again sucked into the lively hustle of the narrow streets, and it is well worth taking Via di S. Martino ai Monti, the last stretch of the climb up to the Esquiline Hill through the very old Clivus Suburanus, which is squeezed between two rows of interesting eighteenth and nineteenth-century buildings. Until 1870, it was called Via della Coroncina because of a small crown placed to adorn an image of the Madonna inside a niche. We then reach a small square embellished by a staircase leading inside the Basilica of San Silvestro and San Martino ai Monti.

Basilica S.Silvestro e S. Martino ai Monti

The church, built around 509, stands on the site where in the third century A.D., there was the Titulus of Equizio, in the region that in the Servian Rome was called "Esquilina" and in the Augustan Rome "Tertia Regio" dedicated to the cult of Isis and Serapis. In this area, remarkable findings were discovered: remains of the Domus Aurea, the Baths of Titus, Trajan and Domitian, the Portico of Livia, the Temple of Isis and Serapis, the fountain of Orpheus and the beech grove with a sacred temple to Jupiter. Equitius was the presbyter or priest who, at the beginning of the 4th century, turned this 3rd-century Roman villa into a place of Christian worship, also using it as a personal residence.

Titolo Equizio (Room 1)

Walking along the entire nave, we reach the altar where we are struck by a singular architectural overlap, which highlights the different functions of the spaces: the Renaissance church, the medieval crypt and the Roman titulus currently accessible from the main staircase.

Inside the titulus, we can still see fragments of tombstones from recent excavations, the remains of palm tree decorations, a column, a frieze with the good shepherd, a tabernacle with cosmatesque decorations and the 9th-century Byzantine fresco of St. Agnes. The domus is divided into eight rooms, each containing important works.

Titolo Equizio (Room 2)

The church is also known as the Basilica of St.Silvestro and has been frequently restored. The original structure of the building was simple; the top of the apse had medallions and masks, and the façade overlooked a small atrium. The high altar was located further than the present one, and below it was a semicircular crypt; inside, there was the cell with the relics of the martyrs and saints brought from the catacombs of Priscilla. The apse catches the visitor's imagination thanks to a rich mosaic, traces of frescoes with prayers and doves resting on flowers and grass. The Basilica, traditionally managed by the Carmelite priests, owes them its current state of excellent preservation. Even the floor was lowered by almost 31 inches, and the plinths of the columns were covered with black marble. The walls of the aisles were decorated with frescoes and the crypt under the high altar has been completely rebuilt. The magical atmosphere of the place is made even more attractive by the cycle of 18 frescoes arranged in the aisles, 16 of which were painted by Gaspare Dughet in the mid-17th century. They are full of light and air, lively in their movements and colours, with an unusual aspect for a sacred place and represent an original decorative element. The subjects treated are the life of the prophet Elijah worshipped as an inspirer for the Carmelites, as well as some of the local religious traditions. The non-religious subjects seem to be a pretext for the artist to capture the enchanting scenery of the Roman countryside, by which he was strongly impressed. Two very prestigious frescoes by Filippo Gagliardi reproduce the interiors of the ancient basilicas of St. Peter's in the Vatican and St. John Lateran, the two major centres of worship for pilgrims. The old convent attached to the basilica, was donated by Pope Boniface VIII to the Carmelite order in 1299.

Before proceeding to Colle Oppio, along Via Merulana, at Largo Leopardi, we are overwhelmed by the impressive Palazzo Brancaccio, the property of an ancient Neapolitan family, built in the years 1892-1896 on the area of the vineyards that once had belonged to the Jesuits and which today hosts both the Museum of Oriental Art and the Brancaccio Theatre.

Palazzo Brancaccio

The garden is extremely interesting, containing the remains of the villa, which had belonged to Mecenate, the counsellor and friend of Emperor Augustus. From its terrace, he could enjoy what was then called “fumum et opes strepitumque Romae” (the frantic life of ancient Rome). He was responsible for the renovation works of the old cemetery pits called ‘puticoli’, outside the ancient Servian “pomerio,” used as a popular burial place. The cemetery pits on the Cispio, the south fringe of the Esquiline, were used for burial and had holes at the top to let gas off. Therefore, the area was particularly smelly, and it was there that Mecenate organised a service of transport of agricultural land, cleaning up the whole area from San Martino ai Monti to Piazza Vittorio Emanuele, eliminating the pits and thus complying with the popular quotation “do quia habeo” (I give what I have) which underlined his generosity to the city.

Porta Esquilina and Arco di Gallieno

Crossing via Merulana from Palazzo Brancaccio, near an old bakery celebrated by gourmets for its high-quality bread and cakes, exactly in the middle of Largo Leopardi is located an old construction which is completely different from the architectural style of the surrounding area, thus arousing curiosity. We pause to examine it, tracing its circular perimeter and trying to guess its original date of construction, until we discover that the monument was part of the luxurious villa of Mecenate and is known today as the Auditorium of Mecenate. It consists of a large hall 13 meters wide and 24 meters long, with a semicircular apse at the bottom that has a staircase consisting of seven narrow concentric steps; the hall was originally underground, and its most striking feature is the pictorial decoration created at the beginning of the first century A.D. on a long frieze against a black background with Dionysian scenes and miniature gardens. The hall was also embellished with water games and was intended as a place for convivial and cultural meetings.

We continue walking along Via Merulana until we reach Piazza San Giovanni in Laterano, where we cannot but stop at the first of the four major basilicas, the oldest and most important one in the Western world. It has a very ancient history and also benefits from extraterritoriality. It is considered the cathedral of Rome and represents the first significant model of a place of worship dedicated to the new Christian religion, which became official in the period following Constantine's victory over Massenzio in 312. Constantine, personally convinced of the positivity of the new faith, wanted it to expand and become a free expression of worship that was no longer persecuted as in the past. Thus, he identified an area that he considered central to the city, arranged for a large space to be used for the construction of a suitable place of worship, and had a large church erected where Christians could gather and pray. Initially, the Christian religion had to coexist with the pagan one, which was still widely followed by the aristocracy living in the Forum.

In Piazza San Giovanni in Laterano stands the world's tallest obelisk (32 meters), transported to Rome from Thebes in the year 357. Its pieces were reassembled in their present form in 1588 by Domenico Fontana, giving the square a great historical and cultural value, worth the solemnity of the basilica. The present façade of the basilica was completed in 1735 by Alessandro Galilei in a classical style that emphasizes verticality, thus achieving an effect of great power due to the height of the columns and the presence of statues arranged along the perimeter of the façade. In the middle, Christ holding a cross is in the act of blessing the crowds; the two side statues of St. John the Evangelist and St. John the Baptist are accompanied by twelve doctors of the Greek and Latin churches. The entire sculptural group looms majestically upward, creating an optical effect of ascending to Heaven. The atrium, simpler than the one in St. Peter's Basilica but similar in structure, houses the large statue of Constantine in a quadrangular niche.

Obelisk in San Giovanni Laterano square

Costantino's statue in San Giovanni in Laterano's porch

There are also 24 white marble pillars with capitals on the porch, and the barrel ceiling highlights the coat of arms of Pope Clement XII (1730). There are five entrances under the porch, and the door on the far right is the Holy Door, opened only during the Jubilees. Then there is the bronze door by Floriano Bodini, commissioned by Pope John Paul II in 2000 and depicting a dead Christ, the Madonna and Child, a blessing hand and the papal coat of arms. The upper part of the porch is adorned with carved slabs depicting scenes from the life of St. John the Baptist. The basilica has a northern facade with the so-called Loggia delle Benedizioni, built in 1586 by Domenico Fontana and commissioned by Pope Sisto V. The loggia is entirely decorated with stories from the Old Testament and paintings of the Virgin, Apostles and Popes. The northern façade is framed by two 13th-century bell towers that replaced the two original medieval towers.

San Giovanni in Laterano Basilica

The strong curiosity to discover the treasures of this vast and majestic church, rebuilt mainly by Francesco Borromini for the 1650 Jubilee, prompts us to enter. The oldest elements, such as the wooden coffered ceiling, coexist with the innovations introduced by Borromini, such as the large shrines of ancient green marble in which the colossal statues of the twelve Apostles are placed. The church has five naves, and the middle one on the right displays one of the greatest jewels, a fragment of a fresco depicting Boniface VIII proclaiming the first Jubilee in 1300, a work that is attributed to Giotto.

Boniface VIII proclaiming the first Jubilee in 1300

On the second pillar on the right, there is a monument dedicated to Sylvester II, linked to a legend according to which the marble plaque exudes water on the occasion of a pope's death. Moving on, we find the monument to Alexander II, an opponent of Emperor Frederick Barbarossa and founder of the Lombard League. In the final part of the nave are two noble chapels, the Orsini and the Torlonia. In the left aisles there is the Adoration Chapel and other noble chapels belonging to the Colonna, the De Rossi, the Antonelli and the Corsini. The white marble altar with mosaic-decorated columns, where all the popes have started their sacred rituals throughout history, has been of great artistic importance. In the two wings of the transept, eight large frescoes painted by Cavalier d'Arpino around 1600 and representing scenes from Constantine's history stand out for their beauty. On the left of the apse, the altar of the Blessed Sacrament is striking for its peculiar structure, topped by a triangular tympanum held up by four large fluted columns in Corinthian style, originating from Roman constructions and recalling an ancient Greek temple. A fragment of cedar wood is placed above the bronze tabernacle, which tradition has attributed to the table on which Jesus and the Apostles dined together for the last time. Everything is crowned by a grand and eventful fresco by Cavalier d'Arpino, portraying the Ascension. The fusion of the two religions is evident: polytheism dating back to pre-Constantine times, which is represented on the altar as a pagan temple, and monotheism portrayed by the frescoes focusing on Jesus Christ. The observer is helped to follow the crucial moment of this transition well represented in the frescoes and mosaics. The newly rebuilt apse was decorated with pre-existing mosaics by Iacopo Torriti, dating back to the late 13th century.

Mosaics in the apse

The images portrayed are those of Christ, placed in the upper part of the mosaic and the Jordan River flowing in the lower part. Below are nine apostles, some Franciscan artists made smaller with their working tools. Beneath the mosaic is the papal chair, which here takes on the function of the Bishop's Chair. On either side of the apse are two gigantic frescoes from the 1800s. The large Baroque organ from 1598, adorned with musician angels, is remarkable. The access to the cloister is on the left aisle, the work of famous marble workers of the 13th century. This small but fascinating hidden corner, characterized by a mystical atmosphere of peace and serenity, takes us back to a distant past, when the essence of monastic life reemerges in a beautiful fresco of the Virgin from the 14th century. The cloister is a masterpiece of cosmatesque architecture, enriched by columns of various shapes with sphinxes and lions, and the perimeter walls are embellished with sculptures, stone and marble slabs dating back to the 13th, 14th and 15th centuries.

San Giovanni in Laterano cloister

As you leave the basilica, you can find the separate building of the baptistery, erected in the first century by Constantine and rebuilt later until it assumed its present aspect under the papacy of Urban VIII in 1637. Not far away, another particular basilica catches our eye: Santo Stefano Rotondo, located in a corner hidden by a large Neronian aqueduct ruin; the very ancient (468), circular-shaped church is inspired by the Holy Sepulchre in Jerusalem, both in shape and size. The structure, composed of three concentric circles in which a Greek cross is inscribed, is supported by granite columns on which both the central archway and the cupola's dome tiburium stand. Thirty-four frescoes follow each other in a sequence on the round walls of the church. They show scenes of martyrdom, commissioned by the Jesuits to make the novices aware of their possible destiny as missionaries in distant lands. The frescoes are painted in bright colours, highlighting cruel details and emphasizing how the missionary's spirit had to be strong and inspired by the iron principles of the Counter-Reformation. Harshness of the frescoes contrasts with the sweetness of the precious original Byzantine mosaics located in the Chapel of Saints Primo and Feliciano.

As we leave the hill and proceed toward the Colosseum on Via dei Querceti, at the corner with Via dei Santissimi Quattro, we notice a small stone image erected to purify the place from a sacrilege about a popular legend, telling that the presumed *"Papessa"* Giovanna had given birth to a son there.

A few steps away, it is worth visiting one of the most beautiful and ancient basilicas in Rome, the Church of St. Clemente, dedicated to the memory of Pope Clement III, a Christian martyr in the imperial times. The place follows the ancient tradition of three overlapping levels; on the lowest level, there are still the remains of public and private Roman buildings, and in one of these rooms, a place of worship, a *mithraeum* was built. At the end of the 4th century, an early Christian basilica with three naves carrying columns was built in the intermediate layer, which was considered important during the Middle Ages. After the destruction caused by the barbarian invasions, the church was initially abandoned and then totally rebuilt over the previous two levels, and in the 1700s, the architectural intervention by Carlo Fontana maintained the medieval layout. The courtyard retains an aspect of great simplicity and mysticism, circled by Ionic columns and architraves that frame the beautiful 18th-century façade. Inside, there are three naves, each ending in its own apse, and later interventions are evident in the panelled ceiling and in the pictorial cycle of the central nave. The ancient columns from Roman remains, and the marvellous cosmatesque floor stand out, not to mention the 12th-century *Schola Cantorum*. The masterpiece in the central apse contains an original mosaic representing Christ crucified between the Virgin and St. John. In the centre, a cross is placed on an acanthus tuft whose golden volutes occupy the entire surface in full Byzantine style, interspersed with numerous figures and symbolic motifs, while in the lower part are portrayed a number of deer drinking from four heavenly rivers flowing from the cross.

In the left aisle is the chapel of St. Catherine of Alexandria, another victim of the cruelty of martyrdom perpetrated by the Romans. Valuable frescoes by Masolino da Panicale in the early 15th century and depicting stories from the lives of St. Catherine and St. Ambrose can be seen there. Access to the lower basilica is through the sacristy. This place, whose roof was lowered to allow the construction of the upper basilica, still presents frescoes from the 9th to the 12th century of unique beauty because it is perfect evidence of medieval painting. From the left aisle we descend further to find ourselves in the Roman rooms, also containing stucco and frescoes and where the original *mithraeum* is also located. Venturing into the underground tunnels, it is possible to glimpse a stream of water that must have once been one of Rome's many waterways.

Leaving this place that concentrates the most significant moments of an artistic evolution, we are in front of the Colosseum, which is the absolute protagonist of this area. From any corner, we can catch a glimpse of its walls, that are a perpetual reminder of the glory and splendour of imperial Rome. The fascination, the magic that it has unleashed over the centuries, continues to amaze today if we just think about the countless devastations to which it was exposed. "It was used as a fortress for invaders and invaded, was burned by barbarians, and became a quarry for building materials. During the civil wars, it was turned into a contended fortress between the two families of Frangipane and Annibaldi. Earthquakes weakened it...yet exposed for so many centuries to destruction, the amphitheatre stood and appeared as indestructible." Its indestructibility gave rise to a popular legend that the Colosseum was to last as long as Rome and as long as the whole world. It was built in Flavian times by Vespasiano and later Titus on the edge of the Roman Forum and was inaugurated on April 21st in the year 80 A.D. It was to exalt and celebrate the power of the Empire and, at the same time, to provide the people with recreation and entertainment. It was called the *Colosseum* because of its exceptional size (48 meters high on a 3358 square meters area) and because of the nearby colossal statue of Nero. It was mainly used for gladiators' fights, public performances and naval battles and could accommodate from 50 thousand to 87 thousand spectators inside. Since 2007, it has been among the new seven wonders of the world. Its complex is an example of a perfect architectural construction, formed by successive arches and vaults generating a gigantic whole that is unique and was once considered the amphitheatre *par excellence*.

The Colosseum

The Colosseum had a roof made of ship sail cloth (velarium) that protected spectators in the stalls from the sun and rain. It was operated by special sailors from the fleet of Misenus, who had their camp not far away, on top of the Celio hill, almost certainly on the site where the Basilica of Santa Maria in Domnica *alla Navicella* was erected in the 5th-6th centuries. Its name is linked to the discovery of a small stone ship from Roman times that can probably be related to the camp of the fleet, and that was turned into a fountain by Pope Leo X in the 16th century. Next to the basilica, a public park tells the story of one of Rome's richest families: the Mattei family. Originally, an extensive vineyard was purchased by the family in the 1500s for a thousand golden scudi. The sumptuous palace overlooking the hill and the garden contains pieces from various historical periods, among which the Egyptian obelisk of Ramesses II. After several events, the mansion was sold by the Mattei family in the 1800s, and in the early 1900s, it was expropriated and made the headquarters of the Italian Geographical Society. The gardens still are an oasis of peace and quietness for those who wish to enjoy the rich greenery.

We end our walk moving up to the park of Colle Oppio, a garden of remarkable beauty in a magical setting, which the ancient Romans had already chosen for its favourable and pleasant location. Nero had built his Domus Aurea there as an example of splendour and opulence filled with beautiful frescoes and fine mosaics, then Traiano chose this place for his Thermal Baths, whose ruins called "the Seven Halls" (probably water supply tanks) bear witness to this. Leaving the peaceful atmosphere of the Colle Oppio park, we are again in the heart of the Monti neighbourhood; we walk up Via dei Serpenti, where a break on the steps of the Madonna dei Monti fountain is almost inevitable, perhaps enjoying a tasty slice of pizza from one of the many renowned bakeries in the area.

On top of the street, we get out into Via Nazionale, the great avenue at the foot of Quirinale Hill. Walking further in the direction of Termini station, we reach Piazza Esedra or Piazza della Repubblica, and here we cannot but be fascinated by the imposing fountain of Naiads, which offers a true scenic sight with its waterworks. Yet when it was built in 1901 by the architect Mario Rutelli, it caused a scandal, especially among the conservative Catholics of papal Rome, who saw an 'outrageous message' in the sensual figures of the four naked Naiads. A wooden gate was built around the circular pool, thus limiting the view of those winding and sensual bronze figures representing the four nymphs of lakes, rivers, groundwater and oceans. The triumph of water gushing from the inner pool to the outer pool and back again creates a misty silvery illusion that offers a dreamlike vision of the mythological figures. On the square is the simple façade of the Basilica of St. Mary of the Angels and Martyrs, a place that shows its own architectural distinctiveness as it was made out of the original *frigidarium* of the Diocleziano's Baths. Michelangelo, who was its first architect in 1561, did not want to alter the original layout, creating a place of worship that was unusually more extensive in width than in length. Vanvitelli's later intervention in 1750 gave the architectural structure a shape more appropriate to the trends of the time, correcting Michelangelo's project. The church was also enriched with precious mosaics instead of paintings, which better suited this place because of the excess humidity. The basilica was the site of the wedding between King Victor Emmanuel III of Savoy and Princess Elena and since then has been consecrated a State church, where funeral ceremonies of Italian Army personalities are held. The vast Baths complex at the back of the basilica hides a jewel of Renaissance architecture, which also proves to be an interesting example of layering: the Michelangelo cloister. From the ancient structure of the Roman Baths, the artist had designed the cloister, which was later built between 1565 and 1676. It is a very large space of quadrangular structure, full of travertine columns and many statues and sarcophagi arranged on the four wings of the cloister, in the centre of which are seven animal heads found near the Trajan Column. There is also the dolphin fountain surrounded by cypress trees.

Leaving Piazza della Repubblica and taking Via XX Settembre, we reach Largo Santa Susanna, where there is the small church of Santa Maria della Vittoria, in which the beautiful Cornaro Chapel stands out, housing a marble and bronze sculpture "The Ecstasy of Santa Teresa," a magnificent example of the Baroque style designed by Bernini in 1652. In the centre of an imaginary stage is placed a scene of moving beauty, narrating the moment when St. Teresa of Avila is pierced with a dart by an angel, receiving her vocation, and experiencing ecstasy that is described as follows in her diary ("Vida") "I saw an angel, near me placed in bodily appearance(....). I saw in his hands a long golden dart, and on the tip, there seemed to me to be a little fire. It seemed to me that sometimes with it, he wounded my heart and penetrated to my bowels: in withdrawing it to himself, it seemed to me that he carried the same with him." As the theatrical scene unfolds, the Cornaro family seems to be really watching from perfectly sculpted side stages, reproducing a kind of performance in which the audience is ideally expected to participate and fully identify with it. Everything resumes the illusion of an imaginary theatrical space, where the main 'actress' shares her emotion at the moment of her dazzling vocation with the audience, keen to grasp the profound emotion evoked by the encounter between the Saint and God.

“Ecstasy of Santa Teresa”

TREVI AND QUIRINALE

"Do you still remember Rome, dear Lou? How is it in your memory? One day, only its waters will remain in mine, these limpid, amazing, moving waters that live in the squares; and the stairs, which seem to be modeled on falling waters, so curiously, one step slides into another like a wave from a wave; the joy of the gardens and the magnificence of the great terraces; the nights so long, silent and full of stars." (Rainer Maria Rilke from his letter to Lou Salome, 3rd Nov.1903). The charm of water is certainly present in every corner of the city: the continuous flowing of the Tiber, the great aqueducts, the imposing fountains and the drinking little ones called "nasoni" scattered here and there to distribute drinking water, with their iron taps in the shape of large noses.

Trevi Fountain has always been a landmark for visitors, who come here from all over the world to throw their coins into the basin, performing an almost ritual gesture that will ensure their return to the eternal city. Even more famous is the well-known scene from the movie "La Dolce Vita" by F. Fellini, in which Anita Ekberg walks inside the pool dressed up in her clothes. The fountain still today remains an icon of the city and bears the name of the surrounding area. It is so called because of the three inlets of the Acqua Vergine trivium water system, built by the Roman architect Agrippa, nephew of Octavian Augustus, in 19 B.C. The trivium is the junction of three streets in the centre of the neighbourhood: Via Poli, Via dei Crociferi and Via di S. Vincenzo. The famous architect had built a new waterway in order to fill the pond with water, located near the present fountain. The story tells that a peasant girl, a Virgo, had shown the source of a stream to soldiers on recognition in the Roman countryside. And it was just this source that, after complex works and the construction of pipes that passed under the Pincio, Piazza di Spagna and via dei Condotti, supplied water to most of this area, also managing to survive the damages caused to the other waterworks by the barbarian invasions.

Trevi Fountain

The fountain stands out in its spectacular proportions, catching the eye of passersby with its majestic dimensions and showing a powerful mixture of mythology, art and nature.

It was commissioned by Pope Urban VIII in 1640 and designed by Gian Lorenzo Bernini, who made it as a simple exedra-shaped base with a pool stretching forward. It was only in 1732 that Pope Clement XIII commissioned the architect Nicola Salvi to build a new, more monumental fountain without worrying too much about the palace behind it. By using a huge covered basin behind the facade of Palazzo Poli, the architect managed to create a much larger arch-shaped project, with a deep niche sloping towards the large basin that opens onto a wide and majestic cliff full of plants where the water flows, producing spectacular effects. In the middle, there is the statue of Ocean driving a shell-shaped chariot, pulled by two horses, the quiet and the wrathful one, handheld by two tritons. Some carved allegorical figures, referring to the beneficial effects of water, recall how the new philosophical currents were emphasising the importance of nature. On either side of Oceano stand two large statues of Abundance and Health, above which two bas-relief panels are placed. One depicts Agrippa intending to start the construction of the new aqueduct; the other depicts the scene in which the virgin shows the soldiers the source of water, "Virgo."

Piazza di Trevi is in the middle of an area made of narrow streets, small squares, simple widening and characteristic corners where the traits of ancient Rome still survive. For example, there is the alley of the Models, a narrow street that starts from Via S. Vincenzo and is famous because most of the women and men who worked as models in the 18th century lived there; they came down to Rome from Ciociaria and Abruzzo and were hired especially by foreign painters who made them pose in their characteristic costumes. The lane ends up in a small square, Piazza Scanderbeg, whose name is related to an Albanese national hero of the first half of the 15th century who used to live there.

Vicolo Scanderbeg

Nearby, there is a long flight of steps via dello Scalone, from which the Quirinale palace rises up in its impressive magnificence and where we have access to via della Panetteria, once famous because bread was prepared for the papal court. Walking down this alley towards Via del Tritone, we stop in front of Palazzo Antamoro, whose sober façade would never suggest the existence of a small courtyard adorned with an imaginative fountain, the work of Gian Lorenzo Bernini. The sense of wonder increases when you meet a group of art restorers engaged in reconstructing the missing parts of the fountain pots with a passion that they communicate to anyone. Towards the end of the 17th century, Paolo Strada, personal valet of Clement IX, had obtained the papal permission to connect the palace to the *Acqua Felice* water pipeline, allowing Bernini to build the fountain. It was designed on three pots topped by two tritons holding a whelk in their right hand and supporting the coat of arms of the Antamoro counts in their left hand.

On the opposite side, there is an alley called Vicolo del Babuccio, so named because of the dialectal term 'babbusso' which refers to a very common bird in the local area. Behind Trevi fountain, in the little square facing the Academy of St. Luca, there is the elegant Carpegna palace, built by Giacomo Della Porta towards the end of the 16th century. It was then purchased by the Carpegna Counts around the middle of the 17th century and was completely enlarged and restored by Francesco Borromini, who expressed his original touch both in the entrance hall and in the famous elliptical ramp. The long corridor atrium presents an alternation of arches and pillars with two lateral columns decorated with fine capitals, from which a garland of laurel leaves runs along the entire arch. In the courtyard, you can see the beautiful central fountain and two ancient sarcophagi used as planters, as well as some statues, including a wounded Achilles and a sculpture by Canova. The palace, historically used as the University of Fine Arts, became in 1939 the seat of the Academy of S. Luca.

Carpegna Palace's courtyard

A recurring feature of all the big cities, that can also be found in Rome, is the evident sign of the forced coexistence between opposing social classes, patricians and plebeians, nobles and commoners, aristocrats and common people, which has generated a positive energy for the organization of social life and the identity of the urban structure. Belonging to such a powerful city like Rome meant accepting a set of shared and necessary rules. Large family palaces were certainly built in the most pleasant and healthy areas but often not far from the beating heart of the popular alleys and small squares. In fact, from the elegant Piazza dell'Accademia di San Luca, we are back in Piazza di Trevi where Via del Lavatore winds its way, animated by a traditional fruit and vegetable market and so-called because of the public fountain leaning against the wall of the Quirinale, ironically called the "Lavatore del Papa". The street became famous for a tavern where Bartolomeo Pinelli, a well-known engraver, painter and ceramist of the 18th century, often used to go.

In the maze of alleys also stands out Vicolo del Forno, which takes its name from a baker who opened his store here at the end of the 19th century. This leads to Vicolo delle Bollette, where two celebrated Roman taverns were once located and that have now become restaurants. One of the two, the old Serafini tavern, owned the building on the corner where a dairy stable once stood, in which the cows were milked in the presence of customers. Today, it is a temple of typical Roman cuisine, satisfying the tastes of both the most refined mouths and the genuine ones of the popular tradition, offering *lasagne, spaghetti alla carbonara, bucatini alla amatriciana, and cannelloni.* In the same area, near the ruins of the Serapis Temple, built by Emperor Caracalla, Vicolo dell'Umiltà and Vicolo Sciarra branch off, and it was just in this place that in the middle of the 16th century, the noblewoman Francesca Baglioni

Orsini bought some old houses, demolished them and commissioned the construction of a large monastery. The annexed church was dedicated to S. Mary of Humility. The nuns who lived in the monastery, mostly from noble families, joined the Dominican rule, according to which humility was considered the highest virtue. Vicolo Sciarra takes its name from the Palestrina branch of the Colonna family, whose palace overlooks via del Corso; reports of that time tell that the alley was originally called "Tre Ladroni" ("Three Thieves") due to the very high price of the wine charged by the owners of an inn. A few steps from this maze of alleys, you reach SS. Apostoli Square, formerly the realm of aristocratic families such as Colonna, Odescalchi and Balestra, shows signs of great architects such as Bernini and Vanvitelli.

"The intense colour of the June sun is different in Rome: I feel the wonder of walking around in a place I had never imagined before, the magical gardens of Casa Colonna, resembling the background of paintings. From Piazza dei Santi Apostoli, the gardens rise in terraces, just as, according to the legend, the gardens of Babylon once climbed. They stretch as far as the Quirinale hill. There is a joyous solemnity, an Olympic happiness in this place that has no equal in its way. The hilly terrain is covered with groves, giant pines, slender cypresses bursting with leafy branches, sumptuously fringed palms, playful orchards, well-cultivated gardens, groves of heather and fountains at every turn. Entire hedges of rose bushes divide the spaces, alternating with huge jasmine bushes that release scents from their starry corollas. Every now and then, gigantic Roman arches, pillars, columns, and sculpted frames are revealed among the greenery, and scholars debate whether they are the ruins of Constantine Baths or the Temple of the Sun." (from "Private Renaissance" by Maria Bellonci 1986).

These detailed descriptions, so harmonically bound together, catch the senses and make us truly experience the magical atmosphere of Palazzo Colonna gardens. In the Renaissance setting recreated by the writer, the scents released by the flowers penetrate the nostrils, the deaf sounds of the birds singing break the silence, and the ancient ruins of the temples dazzle the eye.

Palazzo Colonna gardens

Here we are in front of the magnificent entrance to Palazzo Colonna, which opens onto SS. Apostoli Square and our thoughts immediately jump back to the Rome of the Popes and to the powerful patrician dynasties, among which the Colonna family stands out. Since medieval times, this family has not only limited its power to its own territory but has gained an outstanding reputation and prestige in the history of Italy. The Colonna family, counts of Tusculum, owned a very large area and enjoyed important hereditary titles such as Patrizio Napoletano, Patrizio

Veneto, Gran Connestabile and Prince assistant to the Papal Throne, from which the Latin saying “mole sua stat” (It stands in its greatness). However, since the 14th century, the Colonna family had gained importance and expanded their possessions, provoking hostility and rivalry in other families such as the Caetani, which in 1301 had bought and fortified the nearby Torre delle Milizie in order to contrast their supremacy. The hostility to the Orsini family was political and religious since the two powerful families were opposed to each other in the struggle between the Papacy and the Holy Roman Empire, being the Colonna on the Ghibelline side and the Orsini on the Guelph side. The palace owned by the Colonna family stretched from the Quirinale to Mount Acceptorium, namely Montecitorio, and it was completed under the papacy of Bonifacio VIII at the end of the 13th century. According to the tradition, it stands on the site where Emperor Aurelian had the Temple of the Sun built, having the Syrian temples of Palmyra as a model. The construction was huge and was gradually dismantled and destroyed during the Middle Ages. Later, it was also used as a quarry for marble material until the Renaissance. As early as the 13th and 14th centuries, the Colonnas’ stronghold had included an area used for planting, and after a period of struggles with rival families, the property was transformed into a villa. In the 16th-century maps, the gigantic ruins of the temple can still be seen, inlaid in a completely green area and their remains are today partially visible from the gardens of the residence.

In the 17th century, extensive renovation works were carried out, unifying the various buildings into one single large architectural complex and involving famous artists who contributed to the decoration of the interiors, adding a strong baroque touch. Around 1654, the Colonna Gallery was built, still exists today, and is destined to contain the rich artistic collection of the family, known as one of the most impressive of the city, even though after a period of economic crisis, part of the family's artistic heritage was unfortunately to be alienated, including works by Raphael, Titian, Reni and Veronese. The palace shows grandeur and attention to every single detail, typical of the Baroque style, revealing all the power and magnificence of the noble family. Decorated mirrors, gilded and lavishly elaborated frames, majestic Murano chandeliers, precious ebony caskets, Roman statues and marble inlay floors, imposing paintings by famous painters from Guido Reni, Tintoretto and Botticelli to Veronese, Carracci and Guercino contribute to give the place such a magnificence worth of the great imperial palaces.

Colonna Gallery

Venere Cupido and Satiro by Agnolo Bronzino at Galleria Colonna

Fountain Hall at Palazzo Colonna with the vault frescoed by Pinturicchio

As early as 1328, the residence had hosted Ludwig the Bavarian consecrated Emperor of the Holy Roman Empire, Petrarch in 1341, who stayed there during his poetic coronation in Campidoglio and artists such as Michelangelo, Caravaggio and not least Bernini, who was commissioned the creation of the famous Gallery.

Among the members of the family who have contributed to the history of the country, we can mention Oddone Colonna, who became Pope in 1417 with the name of Martin V and reconciled the Western Schism, bringing back the papal seat from Avignon to Rome, thus promoting an intense economic and cultural growth of the city. The cousins Prospero and Fabrizio Colonna were the protagonists of the Disfida di Barletta (Barletta Battle) in 1503, a clash provoked by thirteen French knights who challenged the Italians, considering them militarily inferior. Thanks to the military strategies and coordination of the Colonna cousins, the thirteen Italian knights, led by Ettore Fieramosca, were able to achieve a crushing victory over the French. Marcantonio Colonna was another hero to be mentioned for the battle of Lepanto in 1571, as well as the poetess Vittoria Colonna, Michelangelo's muse. In 1527, during the Sack of Rome by the Lanzichenecchi of Charles V, the palace that had hosted Isabella d'Este, marchioness of Mantua, was spared the violent raid. Because of her eminent presence, the building was used as a refuge for more than two thousand people who knew how to respect its beauty despite the harsh moment they were living. The garden of the palace extends over three large terraces on the sloping sides of the Quirinale hill. Inside the Italian garden, where the spaces are well separated according to a geometric system of trees and hedgerows, there are three statues, the central one featuring Marcantonio Colonna in the guise of an ancient Roman citizen to emphasize his heroism. There is also a wall fountain on the second level, from which the water flows down along two flights of steps and more tree-lined flowerbeds that end with the majestic entrance. Both the gardens and the palace were famous for their splendid banquets, including that of the "chinea", which consisted in offering a white mule to the Pope on behalf of the King of Naples by his Constable Prince Colonna, in consideration of the link between the Colonna family and the Borboni. This act of submission was celebrated with a sumptuous ceremony.

Via della Pilotta

Indeed, the entire area at the foot of the Quirinal Hill was a sort of feud belonging to the powerful Colonna family as early as 1400. Behind the palace, there was a country lane called Vicus Caprarius, which took its name from a *Roman aedicula* showing a goat that was the symbol of the street. This alley was widened and paved, today is called via della Pilotta, whose name comes from the game of pilotta, the Spanish game of pelota, brought to Rome by the

Florentines and which used to take place in the homonymous square.

Continuing the walk, we reach Vicolo del Monticello, where you can take a suggestive view over S.Maria dell'Umiltà bell tower. From Piazza della Pilotta winds via del Vaccaro, whose name refers to a rich shopkeeper of the street, that traditionally keeps a reference to trades in its name. At the corner with Via di S. Marcello and continuing in the direction of Via dell'Umiltà, you can see the small chapel of the Archetto set between the walls of two buildings, one of them belonged to the Countess Savorelli. It is known because there was a painting of the Virgin, which was said to have miraculously moved her eyes. The countess then made the painting available to the public so that everyone could worship it, and after one hundred years, the Virgin was again seen moving her eyes, remarkably increasing the number of pilgrims.

Vicolo del Monticello

Going up via dei Lucchesi and taking via di Montecavallo, we approach Palazzo del Quirinale, which can be glimpsed in all its grandeur on the way up. Before reaching the homonymous square and observing the palace in its details, it is worth remembering the origin of its name, which derives from the temple dedicated to Romulus Quirinus, built around 300 B.C. and recalling the origins of Rome. The hill, initially inhabited by tribes of Sabines, was very ancient and constituted one of the first urban nuclei of the city. It occupied a high ground, whose peak was located in the so-called Capitolium Vetus. In 1574 Pope Gregory XIII commissioned the architect Mascherino the construction of a holiday residence on the top of the hill due to its balsamic air. Thus, the first structure of the palace was erected exactly on the ruins of the Baths of Constantine, and the part called "Manica Lunga" hid the remains of the pagan temple dedicated to the god Quirino, so much adored by the Sabines. Great artists and all the architects working for the popes, from Humanism to Renaissance and Baroque, contributed to its construction, which lasted half a century and planned an extension of the city from the area of Campomarzio up to the Quirinale Hill, which was finally requalified as an urban area. In 1587, Pope Sixtus V placed in the square in front of the palace the two Dioscuri, Roman copies of Greek original statues, and between the two giants, he wanted a fountain supplied by the water from Acquedotto Felice. At the end of the 18th century, the obelisk from the Mausoleum of Augustus was placed between the two Dioscuri. In 1818 Pope Pius VII installed the present fountain, taken from a huge basin originally in the Roman Forum and used as a drinking pool for livestock.

"From Piazza del Quirinale, or better from Montecavallo, you can see the boundless Ocean of domes, spires and columns that represent the city of Rome. On a white marble pedestal stands a red

granite obelisk piercing the blue sky. In front of it is a large porphyry basin, from the centre of which rises a column of pure water, which gathers together all the colours of the sky, breaking them into a thousand prisms and gradations of shadows, which fall down together with impetuous sprays into the outer basin... The statues of Castor and Polucis stand on elevated pedestals, each in the act of taming his horse...these figures mix together the irresistible energy with the sublime and perfect beauty that should have belonged to the divine nature. The reins are no longer there, but the position of the hands and the sustained, calm and determined gaze, seem to require no mechanical aid to compel obedience....No mould can convey the sublime and living majesty of their limbs and bearing that stand out against the blue Italian sky, and dominate the city of Rome." From P. B. Shelley "Letter to Thomas Love Peacock" 23rd March 1819.

Via dello Scalone

Visiting the Palazzo del Quirinale is a unique experience. Even the triumphal entrance overlooking the opposite large square, carefully supervised by stout guards and not accessible to visitors, suggests a past of splendour and power. Today it is reserved to the President of the Republic, while the side entrance on Via del Quirinale is used by visitors. The entrance to the large courtyard of honour is a large porticoed square of harmonious appearance that overlooks a double loggia topped by a tower. This constituted the original nucleus of the villa, which was to be enlarged several times and by various interventions between the end of 'the 16th century and the beginning of the 17th century. Pope Sisto V had already extended the surface of the palace, commissioning the architect Domenico Fontana to build the long wing facing the square, but it was only with Pope Paolo V Borghese that the palace was finally completed, first by the architect Flaminio Ponzio and then by Carlo Maderno, who created the most famous rooms, such as the papal apartments, the Paolina Chapel and the Corazzieri Hall. In 1639, Pope Urban VIII Barberini contributed to the enlargement of the palace by entrusting Bernini with the realization of the Loggia delle Benedizioni (Loggia of Blessings), which overlooks the square in front of the palace and by purchasing neighbouring lands to embellish the gardens. He also had a wall built around the entire perimeter of the palace and a low defensive tower with embrasures for cannons. Bernini, a versatile artist in vogue with the Barberini family and therefore protected by Pope Urban VIII, confirmed his generous talent even with subsequent popes. In fact, he had started the construction of the "Manica Lunga" (the long sleeve) under the papacy of Alexander VII, continued by the architect Alessandro Specchi in 1722-24 and finished by Ferdinando Fuga in 1732. Between historical news and the slow and rhythmical pace of the military surveillance patrols, the visit proceeds towards the Stairway of Honor, built in 1609 with a double-crossed ramp to allow visitors direct access to the Corazzieri Hall and the Ball Room. This solution was very functional as it prevented the guests from crossing the other halls used mainly as the pope's private apartments. At the intersection of the ramps, you can admire the marvellous fresco by Melozzo da Forlì, dating back to 1480 and representing Christ the Redeemer in glory among the angels.

Corazzieri Hall

Thus, we come to the Corazzieri Hall, from which a sequence of countless rooms unfolds, each linked in terms of furnishings, frescoes and decorations both to the era of the popes and to the short Napoleonic period where clear signs of Napoleon's desire to adapt the rooms to his own imperial needs, are visible in Alexander VII Gallery. When, in 1871, King Vittorio Emanuele II chose the palace as his official residence, the person who perhaps left a mark of her personality on it was Queen Margherita, Umberto I's wife. By her will, the room of Augustus requested by Napoleon became the Throne Room; the original core of the palace used for the papal apartments was transformed in order to meet the needs of the royal family. You pass through the brightly coloured and warm living rooms, the private apartments of the royal lavishly decorated with fine fabrics wrapping massive four-poster beds, enriched by chandeliers from the Venini factory in Venice, coffered ceilings in decorated wood, French tapestries, polychrome marble floors. A reading corner elegantly decorated with a wall shelving of precious ebony is particularly charming. Crossing the Ballroom, originally the ancient hall of the Consistory and the splendid Hall of Mirrors, it seems as if we were listening to a waltzer that drags us into a whirling dance, sucked in by luminous mirrors that instantly generate a multiplying effect of the moving image. Continuing to explore the palace, we pass through the Hall of Cerimonies, the Hall of Virtues, the Hall of the Flood, the Hall of the Loggias, the Hall of the Bussolanti which also contains a copy of Raphael's famous painting "Madonna of the Chair", the Yellow Room, the Hall of Augustus, the Hall of the Ambassadors, the Mascarino Staircase that inspired the architect Borromini for the creation of his elliptical staircase in Palazzo Barberini, the Loggia d'Onore, the Bronzino's Hall, the Passaggetto of Urbano VIII, a small private corridor with 17th century frescoes representing views linked to the Barberini Papacy, the President's Studio, the Music Room, Piffetti's Library, the Victory Room, the Peace Room, the Room of the Bees, celebrating the Barberini coat of arms and the Imperial apartments.

Piffetti's library

All the rooms are bright, and from every window, you can enjoy a unique and spectacular view of the city. Some rooms are embellished with frescoes by G.Lanfranco and A.Tassi and the sumptuous Chapel of the Annunziata with frescoes by Guido Reni. In the Pauline Chapel, next to the Corazzieri Hall, commissioned by Paul V Borghese, inspired by the Sistine Chapel, you can see the splendid decoration of the vault with white and golden stucco and the multi-coloured marble floor, both dating back to the 17th century. Since 1948, the palace has become the residence of the President of the Republic, although not all the successive heads of State have lived there, due to the restoration of important works of art rearranged during the Napoleonic period and the façades restored to their original travertine colour.

The President's Desk

The entrance to the first room offers a series of images of presidents and amazing handwritten letters from famous people, such as Queen Elizabeth II, sultans, presidents and ambassadors. They seem to speak to us of our most recent history full of hope, promise and commitment. It is the place where agreements have been made, treaties signed and alliances sanctioned. It becomes more familiar when we stand in front of the large, simple presidential desk, the one that sees presidents at work promoting actions for the growth and improvement of the nation in a sober setting of refined elegance.

Quirinale Gardens

Although steep and hard to reach, the Quirinale Gardens are an authentic wonder. In the period when the property was temporarily inhabited by Ippolito d'Este it was further enlarged and embellished with rare plants, tree architectures, the maze, statues and inscriptions.

Gregorio XIII Boncompagni divided the gardens into two different areas: the first in Italian style with flower beds, avenues and hedges geometrically arranged, and the second one was left to the state of a forest and called "Silva Estentium". Between the late 16th century and the beginning of the 17th century, Pope Clemente VIII Aldobrandini had the whole garden renovated, thus giving it the look of a royal villa with springs and elegant water games, including the fountain of the organ, built by Giovanni Fontana in 1596. It was also known as the Parnassus Villa because it was originally embellished with muses sculptures taken from a basin in the Estense garden. There, a large nymphaeum dominates, accessible by three fan-shaped staircases, which highlight the considerable rise between the ground floor of the palace and the lower floor of the gardens. The walls and the vault are decorated with stuccoes inspired by mythological as well as Old Testament episodes. At the sides of the niche, two rectangular rooms were used to provide refreshment. The architect Carlo Maderno carried out additional works and traced out the current boundaries with a wall, introducing the canons of the English garden, which implied more natural effects. Inside the garden, there is a building designed by Ferdinando Fuga in the 18th century, consisting of a small loggia that overlooks the Pincio Hill and preserves famous paintings framed by white and golden stuccos. Under the papacy of Innocent XIII, the Quirinale Stables were built by Alessandro Specchi next to the Villa Colonna. The Quirinale Palace is the only one in the world that, for almost half a millennium, has been associated with the idea of political power: the palace of the popes since 1583, the residence of the kings of Italy since 1870 and the seat of the highest office of the Republican State since 1946.

Once out of the Quirinale Palace you can reach Via XX Settembre and, a short distance away, another famous residence, Palazzo Barberini. What splendour and magnificence in these Roman palaces! They marked ages of fame and glory and were chosen not only by the popes but also by the powerful families who sought beauty and offered it to the city. A particularly striking corner is the one characterized by the presence of four fountains, made in the homonymous street by Pope Sixtus V between 1588 and 1593.

They adorn the four corners of the intersection between Via XX Settembre and Via IV Fontane and are set in rectangular niches carved into the four buildings. They represent two male figures, allegories of the Tiber and Arno, placed in front of two female figures embodying Diana and Juno. Once again, water is the protagonist in the sculptures that personify rivers and deities related to them in a play of allegories and symbols. The fountains were built by neighbouring landowners, who obtained their supply from the Felice aqueduct. The intersection marks the conjunction of three different districts: Monti, Trevi and Castro Pretorio.

The urbanization of the area, resulting from the construction of the Felice aqueduct and Via Quattro Fontane in the 16th century, conferred a more city-like aspect to the residence, which had originally belonged to the Sforza family, was then in 1625 bought by the Barberini family who moved there from the palace in Via dei Giubbonari in Campo Marzio, as they wanted to show off their growing importance. The Barberini Palace was designed by Gian Lorenzo Bernini, who took over the direction of the work on Maderno's death in 1629. The young Borromini also worked in the open worksite and is attributed with the helicoidal staircase based on a classical model. Bernini had imagined the construction of two bodies joined by a central section for which he had projected the glass loggia façade, supported by the deep porch, that was to replace the classic courtyard. Such a grandiose palace responded to the wishes of Urban VIII Barberini, who wanted his Florentine family to have a palace that was equal to the residences of the great Roman nobility.

The visitor's imagination is captured by the large hall, whose vault, decorated by Pietro da Cortona, with a fresco of 500 square meters completed in 1639, represents the triumph of the Divine

Providence, a metaphor for the greatness of the Barberini family and highest expression of the baroque style in Rome. Their coat of arms containing three bees on a blue background, originally three horseflies, has long been a symbol of the family's widespread power. They can be seen in large numbers on all the works of art created by Bernini, who thus celebrated the rise and expansion of Pope Urban VIII Barberini.

Divine Providence Hall at Barberini Palace

The decorations of the halls and salons consist of collections of ancient sculptures, which, while referring to classical themes, conform to the Baroque scheme. Particularly noteworthy is the rich collection of paintings, among which stands out "La Fornarina" by Raphael, which still tells us the deep feeling that the artist had for Margherita Luti, the young daughter of the Trastevere baker.

The present façade is the one facing Via IV Fontane, while originally there were two entrances to the building, one more representative on Piazza Barberini and the other lateral on Via IV Fontane, which introduced the private residence or villa. In the 17th century, the main entrance passed through the baroque theatre built by Pietro da Cortona. Both the entrance to the palace from the square and the theatre were demolished in 1932 for the opening of Via Barberini.

The impressive courtyard known as the Cavallerizza, the large doorway of the main façade and the quadrangular staircase by Bernini are of considerable artistic value.

Borromini's staircase at Barberini Palace

Half of the palace was reserved for a secular branch of the family, whose major representative was Taddeo Barberini, who became related to the Colonna family. The opposite and symmetrical wing was instead inhabited by the cardinals of the Barberini family. The gardens were enriched with rare plants, secret courtyards, and Italian-style hedges so as to be considered a place of delight, where the enjoyment of nature was combined with the pleasure of the rich collection of classical sculptures. Cardinal Francesco Barberini, a learned man and one of the first members of the Lincei Academy, was particularly concerned with the arrangement of the garden—both as a place dedicated to the close relationship between man and nature and for the specific botanical interest. This is the reason why rare plants such as the Lisbon orange tree or the Indian yellow jasmine adorned the well-kept spaces rich in flowers and plants from all over the world.

Barberini Palace's Gardens

With our eyes full of the varying greenery of the great palaces gardens, their exotic plants and trees, of the art that oozes out of every single stone in all its forms, we recall Henry James's words, who knew this city well and loved it so much.

"She had long before this taken old Rome into her confidence, for in a world of ruins, the ruin of her happiness seemed a less unnatural catastrophe. She rested her weariness upon things that had crumbled for centuries and yet still were upright; she dropped her secret sadness into the silence of lonely places, where its very modern quality detached itself and grew objective so that as she set in a sun-warmed angle on a winter's day, or stood in a maudy church to which no one came, she could almost smile at it and think of its smallness. Small it was, in the large Roman record, and her haunting sense of the continuity of the human lot easily carried her from the less to the greater. She had become deeply, enderly acquainted with Rome; it interfused and moderated her passion" (Chapter 49 from The Portrait of a Lady by H.James)

CAMPO MARZIO AND RIONE COLONNA

Piazza del Popolo

Visiting Rome would be almost impossible without passing through the neighbourhoods of Campo Marzio (Mar's field) and Colonna. They correspond to the historic centre that includes some of the city's most iconic sights: the great squares of Piazza del Popolo and Piazza di Spagna, the churches, Via del Corso, Via Ripetta, Via Margutta and the aristocratic palaces, the cafes where part of public life took place, the places of power, which were transformed over time yet always bearing the symbols of the great noble families, the signs of the passage of emperors, kings, popes, dictators and politicians. So much history is present in the neighbourhoods that are now famous for leisure and shopping.

It is almost impossible to imagine that in Roman times, during the Republic, the area of Campo Marzio was basically an unhealthy and swampy place because of the continuous flooding of the Tiber. It was not until Emperor Augustus that the land drainage of the marsh between Colonna Square and the Pantheon took place, and temples and monumental public buildings were consequently built up to Via in Lucina, where a sundial stood. In that place, there was a grove called Augustus's Grove, leading to his great Mausoleum, which was transformed by the powerful families who would acquire it. It became a fortress under the Colonna family, a ruin with Boniface VIII, a burial place in the 1500s, a circus with the Corea family, and then a popular theatre in the 1700s. A very large square obtained by demolishing old neighbourhoods and streets such as Via degli Schiavoni, piazza Augusto Imperatore was named after Augustus, who had his sepulchral mausoleum built nearby, later called the "rotten tooth" because of its bad condition. It was built after the model of Etruscan tombs with a cone-shaped mound planted with cypresses and bearing a statue of the emperor. Inside, the entire family was buried, including his sister Octavia and his nephew Marcellus, as well as his faithful general Agrippa, the architect of many important works of urban improvement. Popular rumours say that this area is teeming with the ghosts of all the people buried there, including the revolutionary Cola di Rienzo. What remains of the Mausoleum was called "Corea" after the name of the noble family that had used it as an amphitheatre in the 18th century, where bullfights and bull jousts were held, inspiring the engraver Bartolomeo Pinelli. Today, in front of the mausoleum stands a huge cubic glass building that houses the most significant symbol of the Augustan Empire, the Altar of Peace known as Ara Pacis, built in the 9th century B.C., originally placed in the area of Campus Martius and consecrated to the celebration of the Emperor's military victories. This monument is a symbol of the peace and prosperity achieved during the happy period of Augustus' empire.

The ancient port of Ripetta was located on the site of the mausoleum, a river port whose function was to ease the arrival of goods that were crowding the port of *Ripa grande*, located south of the city. Later, Porto Clementino, or the port of Ripetta, was redesigned in 1703 by Alessandro Specchi, commissioned by Pope Clement XI. It was built with travertine and the final architectural complex was of great visual effect, value and originality. Its shape, as evidenced in prints by Van Wittel, Piranesi, and Falda, remembered Borrominian architecture in the form of a semicircle with columns and a flight of steps with a cliff-like fountain in the centre. There was also a lighthouse at the top, a reminder of the river function of the port placed in the centre of Rome. You can imagine the grand staircase crawling with people of all kinds and from all over the world moving in an endless rhythm of landings and loading of goods and barrels, just as life must have been in the eighteenth century. The city overlooked the river and offered an animated show of people and boats just under the walls of the Church of San Rocco, wanted by the homonymous Confraternity in 1499, founded on the site where once stood also the hospice built to aid plague victims. Nothing remains of the entire monumental harbour complex as it was destroyed when works were carried out on the Tiber banks in 1889.

The area of the Campo Marzio was originally dedicated to Mars, the god of war and duels, but the vast, open, flat space with its grassy ground, crowned by hills, became in the Augustan period the ideal setting for a sacred place for military and sporting exercises, "necessary for the running of chariots and horses and for that great multitude who used to exercise at the ball, the discus, and the gymnasium," unlike the earlier period when the unhealthy place was used mainly for burials. Around this cleared sacred area, the close distance to the Tiber and the presence of woods and gardens meant that a varied scenery of sumptuous temples and monuments, porticoes, theatres and amphitheatres developed, *"giving a sight that man cannot turn away from without regret"* (Strabone 65 B.C).

Gaspar van Wittel "Tevere al Porto di Ripetta" (sec.XVIII)

The porticoes built by Agrippa, the great architect of Augustus, in the area between the current Via del Corso and Via del Tritone, formed the gathering place for the worldly celebrities of the time, poets and artists, public and distinguished men as well as powerful citizens. According to Vitruvio, author of a prized treatise on ancient architecture, the porticoes were meant to provide protection from the rain, and for people who tended to live outdoors, they also met a social need, namely, to stroll, chat about public affairs and private interests. Conferences were held there, time was spent in a varied and pleasant way, as hundreds and hundreds of years later would be done in cafes, public villas and covered galleries.

An imaginary itinerary in this area could start from Porta del Popolo, which dates back to the 3rd century and is embedded in the Aurelian Walls. It takes its name from the nearby church and has undergone various transformations over time. From an initial structure consisting of two side towers, it was then reduced to a single archway in medieval times. In the 16th century, it was a key entrance into the city, travelling from the north along via Flaminia, and was, for many travellers, the much-desired arrival after exhausting journeys. The last architectural interventions that still remain today date back to that period; the exterior façade was commissioned by Pope Pius IV to Michelangelo in 1562, but the work was carried out by other hands based on his designs that were inspired by the Arch of Titus. The structure is completed by the four columns coming from the ancient St. Peter's Basilica in the Vatican, and the two statues of Peter and Paul displayed in the Basilica of San Paolo were considered too ugly for that church and therefore rejected. The inner façade is a later work and was commissioned by Pope Alexander VII Chigi to Bernini for the arrival of Queen Christina of Sweden on December 23rd, 1655, to whom the welcome inscription was dedicated and which would be a sign of hospitality in the city. The idea that a European queen, daughter of King Gustavus Adolphus, called "defender of Protestantism," would convert to Catholicism represented for the Church of Rome a form of political-religious propaganda and a message for Northern Europe.

Then we enter the beautiful Piazza del Popolo, known throughout the world as symbol of the city for its monumental splendour, created by the perfect symmetry of space, highlighted by the presence of the magnificent obelisk, a fertility symbol of earth and good harvests. It was anciently dedicated to the Sun and was carried by Augustus to Rome after the Egyptian campaign. Twenty-five meters high, made of red granite, it bears an inscription dedicated to the Emperor, and over the centuries, has suffered various ups and downs, including its destruction during the barbarian invasions, only to be rebuilt by Pope Sixtus V in the late 16th century. As a means of emphasizing the slant of the obelisk and adding more value to this unique monument of ancient Egypt, in the late eighteenth century, under Napoleon's rule, plans were made to give the square a new layout. A project carried out by architect Valadier made the space more harmonious by adding the two side hemicycles, one under the Pincio and the other near the Tiber, enriched with sumptuous fountains. To make it even more impressive, in the middle of the square, the The Lions' Fountain, also by Valadier in 1823, replaced a 16th-century fountain with a more flamboyant structure consisting of four basins, adorned with stone lions that recall the style of the obelisk.

The flourishing Pincio Hill, with its lush gardens and vegetable orchards, must have been a marvellous sight that contributed to making the whole area unique. It is the site where Emperor Claudius chose his home, and we wonder, "did the nuns of Trinità dei Monti know that in the place of their chaste thoughts, of their unconscious strolls, Claudio's ill-famed wife, Messalina used to take pleasures and made her passions quiver?" During the Napoleonic period, it was called the "Garden of the Great Caesar" and was remodelled according to the French style, imposed by Napoleon with the intervention of French architects and later redesigned by Valadier, who also planned the Casina Valadier, created as a fashionable meeting place in the neoclassical style with ionic columns and Pompeian frescoes and sculptures. The large green space was destined to the people of Rome as a recreational place, and here we find a curious water-powered clock designed by a Dominican friar. The large terrace overlooking Piazza del Popolo was and still is a corner from which we can enjoy the most enchanting view of the city. In the garden, there is a large collection of marble busts mainly commissioned by Giuseppe Mazzini in 1849, after the Roman Republic, including non-Catholic characters such as Caius Gracchus, Machiavelli, Leopardi, and even an atheist like Vittorio Alfieri. When Pope Pius IX returned to the Vatican from exile, he ordered the renaming of all busts dedicated to heretics, atheists and revolutionaries as they were hostile to the Church.

What changes have occurred over time to create all the charm and beauty that Piazza del Popolo still owns today? After the dark period of the Middle Ages, when this place was mostly marshy because of the constant flooding of the Tiber, perhaps the *Chiesa del Popolo*, built in 1099, is the first step in a series of artistic and architectural changes that have made the square one of the most beautiful and iconic places in the world. The wicked Emperor Nero is said to have chosen this corner of Rome for his own burial, and then Pope Pasquale II commissioned the first stone of the Madonna altar to banish the gloomy ghosts associated with the cruel emperor. A church was erected by the Roman people around this altar, therefore called the Church of the People. About the name "Popolo", there is also another hypothesis, namely that it may be related to dense groves of poplars (populus) in this area. The church today Basilica of Santa Maria del Popolo, is an authentic museum. It contains works of great Renaissance and Baroque artists, such as Raphael who designed and built the Chigi Chapel, commissioned by the wealthy banker Agostino Chigi (1513) and later restored by Bernini. There are frescoes such as "The Birth of the Virgin" by Sebastiano del Piombo and "Jesus and the Samaritan Woman" by Lorenzetto, while the ones in the choir and those in the Rovere Chapel enriched with the masterpiece "The Nativity of St. Jerome" are by Pinturicchio. The Cerasi Chapel is special, showing the "Assumption of the Virgin" by Annibale Carracci on the altar, on the left "the Conversion of St. Paul" and on the right "the Crucifixion of St. Peter" both painted by Caravaggio. There are also contributions from foreign artists who, in the Baroque period, under the guidance of Bramante, embellished the church with decorated stained glass windows illustrating the stories of the Virgin and the childhood of Jesus. Magnificent funerary monuments and prominent marble sculptures enrich the interior.

"Pincio" hill from Piazza del Popolo

The twin churches in Piazza del Popolo and the *Tridente*

The twin churches triumphantly welcome the visitor as to emphasize the entrance into the sacred place of Catholicism. They form the watershed of the Trident, Via del Corso, Via del Babuino and Via di Ripetta. Santa Maria in Montesanto, which borders Via del Babuino, and Santa Maria dei Miracoli, which faces Via di Ripetta, were commissioned by Pope Alexander VII, who had assigned the design to Carlo Rainaldi, to be later completed by Bernini and Carlo Fontana. The perspective effect can be deceptive because the two churches from a distance look like twins, yet for architectural needs, Santa Maria dei Miracoli's dome is actually dodecagonal whereas Santa Maria in Montesanto's is octagonal, although both domes appear slender thanks to their tall drums. The church of Santa Maria in Montesanto is better known as the artists' church and contains the precious painting of the Madonna of Montesanto, where a signature on the back was discovered only through a recent restoration. It belongs to the "silent but revolutionary" painter Plautilla Bricci, the first 17th-century female architect, whose name is related to an unusual episode about the long and laborious work. In a moment of discouragement in painting the Madonna's face, the artist is said to have laid down her paintbrush, and after a short rest, she had found a perfectly sketched face. The church of Santa Maria dei Miracoli (St. Mary of the Miracles) is so named because it is linked to an event that occurred during an overflow of the Tiber in 1325, when a mother, seeing her son fall into the river, turned to the image of the Virgin painted on the wall nearby, and there the miracle of the boy's recovery occurred. A chapel was erected on that site, which was later transformed into the present church. Via del Corso is an ideal continuation of Via Flaminia and is the main road of the Trident.

Via del Corso to Piazza del Popolo

Originally called "via Lata," about a mile long, it is now the most important street in the centre. It was called "corso" in 1466 because of the Barbary horse races held there until the last century, eventually suspended due to an accident. After the regicide in 1914, it was renamed Corso Umberto I, while in 1946, it resumed its original name. The street had been the site of carnival processions and was particularly cared for by the popes until Pio IX, who had it lit entirely by gas in 1854. There were merchants of all kinds "the butchers, the tripe sellers, liver sellers, goat sellers, fryers and poultry sellers" both in stores and on the street until a bill ordered them all to leave the field to fashion stores, tailors, bookstores, antique dealers and jewellers. After the sixteenth century, the street was embellished with noble palaces, becoming a social and meeting place for intellectuals, politicians and artists with time. In the twentieth century, it was also used for car races, "le trottate," organized by prominent figures such as Prince Massimo, Count Tacchia, and King Umberto himself. Nobles, officers and aristocratic ladies watched the races from characteristic cafes such as the historic "Aragno." A curiosity tells that the street was paved by using the taxes paid by the "curiali" or prostitutes. Foot races of Jews, youths, cripples, hunchbacks and prostitutes were also organized there—an unfortunate part of its history. Artists and celebrities such as Cavalier d'Arpino, Luigi Bonaparte, and Wolfgang Goethe lived there. Alongside the street, which has become more and more fashionable, the palaces of the most important Roman families follow each other, almost as if they were competing in a contest of architectural perfection and harmony. Great architects, sculptors and artists have left their signatures on these dwellings, and among them, we come across the beautiful and majestic Palazzo Rondinini, an example of late 18th-century architecture built by Cavalier d'Arpino on a design by Flaminio Ponzio. It has twin portals that serve as the entrance to what was originally a museum, rich in statues marbles and with a beautiful fountain fitted with three niches housing Apollo, Bacchus and Venus. A typical 18th-century taste inspired Piranesi in his renovations and arrangement of the palace's valuable ancient remains. Inside the courtyard stands an obelisk on the top of which a swallow twirls, the symbol of the Rondinini family.

The next building that displays its grandeur on Via del Corso is Palazzo Ruspoli, erected in 1556 by Bartolomeo Ammannati and containing a monumental staircase consisting of one hundred marble steps. The palace belonging to Doria Pamphilj, a family that finds its origin in the union of the Roman Pamphilj with the Genoese Doria, is particularly remarkable. This gigantic building dates back to the 15th century was owned by various noble families such as Della Rovere, Aldobrandini and later the Pamphili, whose descendants still live there. Its quadrangular courtyard with two rows of arcades supported by slender columns with Doric capitals is especially valuable. Over time the building underwent extensions directed by important architects, even boasting the contribution of Bramante, the probable author of the ground floor, and a sumptuous gallery rich in a collection of important works of art can be found in its rooms. Along the same street is Palazzo Bonaparte, purchased in 1818 by Letizia Ramolino, Napoleon's mother, and built in the late 17th century with features that are both Baroque and Renaissance. It is decorated with taste and elegance that emerge in its frescoed rooms and halls where elaborate patterns, rosettes and bright colours prevail. It is also characterized by the presence of a little green balcony called "bussolotto," from which Mrs. Letizia used to observe people strolling along Via del Corso.

Gabriele D'Annunzio described the street as follows:

"The Corso is a long sunny river, a soft golden river into which bodies plunge with voluptuousness. Along the via del Corso, the Tiberian ladies pass, at the weary trot of horses, stretched out in half-closed carriages; and they are pale, mostly hidden by a thick veil, sunk in the softness of furs....

A fierce wind of joy blew down the Corso from the Piazza di Venezia to the Piazza del Popolo; and in the wind, all the multicolored draperies of the balconies swayed, and the popular tide moved in a storm" (G. D'Annunzio).

The street is not only a gallery of aristocratic palaces, beautiful churches embellish the place. Santa Maria in via Lata, with its harmonious façade built by Pietro da Cortona in the mid-17th century, stands on an ancient Roman site that is said to have been St. Paul's prison. Next to the ancient Hospital of the Incurabili is the church of San Giacomo in Augusta, which was finished by Carlo Maderno in 1600. A few steps away, you can spot the mansion that was Canova's home and studio recognizable for its decorative details, made up of fragments of ancient statues and architraves. "Jesus and Mary's Church" is another Baroque church in Via del Corso which offers visitors its precious façade by Carlo Rainaldi.

Canova's home and studio

Then you will be walking again in Via del Corso through the many side streets that are worth exploring, as they all have common aspects and lovely small houses. By the side of the Church of the Miracles in Piazza del Popolo, the second street of the *Tridente* was designed in 1518 by Raphael and Antonio da Sangallo the Younger, according to the old monumental traces, to replace the ancient imperial street that connected Via Flaminia to the port of Ripetta, a lively place animated by traffic. Hosts, wood sellers, and fishermen found this route more convenient than the parallel Via Lata. Via Ripetta, wanted by Pope Leo X, was called Via Leonina, while previously it had been simply nicknamed "ortaccio," because it was wild and untidy and, many prostitutes lived there. By symmetry on the other side of the square, completing the *Tridente,* Via del Babuino was built on the site of the ancient alley that ran along the Pincio to the Quirinale. During the Holy Year 1525, the street called *Clementina,* was in fact, laid out after the homonymous pope. Later renamed Via Paolina, it finally took on its name "Babuino," as it was linked to a statue of Silenus, considered so ugly by the Roman people who called it "er babuino". Only one cardinal assigned the statue a special, almost sacred value since he used to bow and remove his hat in its presence. This stirred the irony of the people who, being used to denigrating the statue, began to post epigrams and invectives against the arrogance of power on it, thus recalling "Pasquino." The Hotel de Russie, located on Via del Babuino, was built in the early 19th century by the Torlonia family and commissioned to the architect Valadier. The building, which was also painted by William Turner during one of his visits to Rome, has always aroused great fascination and attraction among tourists from all over the world. Behind it, there is a secret garden designed by Valadier with spiral staircases that climb up to the Pincio.

This is also the area of the many famous people such as Salvator Rosa, Goethe, Poussain, Trilussa and Riccardo Wagner, who lived here over the centuries, giving it a special artistic and literary value that would last for more than a century until the years of Moravia, Pasolini and many others who continued the tradition of meeting in the cafes of Piazza del Popolo. Continuing the walk, one of the first small streets on the left is Via Margutta, known as the place of art galleries and, over the centuries, has always maintained this strong imprint, described by Winkelmann as a street *"of noble simplicity and quiet grandeur."* Craft stores and antique workshops, framed by a series of lush ivy and wisteria plants, contributes to the attractive and original atmosphere.

In the past, it was a simple street overlooked by aristocratic palaces that had their magnificent entrances on Via del Babuino, while at the back were concentrated stables, mason's stores and stonemasons' workshops that carried out their simple activities. In medieval times, a craftsman began to make portraits and landscape paintings in his workshop, thus attracting the curiosity of many Dutch and Flemish artists and painters, who began to settle on this street in the following centuries. The peak of this flow of painters, musicians and men of letters occurred especially after the nineteenth century when Monsignor Francesco Saverio De Merode had the area cleared, making it particularly attractive to artists, who turned it into an increasingly lively and culturally animated place. Among them, we can mention Picasso, Guttuso, De Chirico, the musicians Wagner, Lisz and Mascagni, and the writers Zola, D'Annunzio, Sartre, Elsa Morante and Sibilla Aleramo. Street number 51 is particularly well known because it was the location where one of the most famous scenes from the movie "Roman Holiday" was filmed, in which the protagonist Audrey Hepburn is charmed by the magical atmosphere. Even today, walking down the street, it may happen to you to chat with the doorkeeper of the building, who eagerly tells about the glories of the *Dolce Vita.* In the early 1950s, some painters launched the fashion of the Art Fair, hanging their paintings on the street walls. Since then the association "One Hundred Painters via Margutta" has given life to a lively exhibition held regularly twice a year in spring and fall. Vicolo degli Orti di Napoli (Naples Gardens Alley) branches off from Via Margutta to Via del Babuino, so-called, both because the artistic academy wanted by King Charles III was located here, housing two architects, two painters and two sculptors from Naples, and because until the 16th century, the area was mainly filled with orchards and vineyards.

Via Margutta

Plaque dedicated to Federico Fellini and Giulietta Masina

The street reconnects to Via del Babuino through Vicolo Alibert, a name taken from the homonymous family that had its home and its own theatre there, which in the 1700s lived its period of fame like many theatres in Rome. Walking up Via del Babuino to the end, a spectacular view opens up over what is the *piazza-scrigno* that includes highlights like piazza di Spagna. Since the 1500s, the large space was intended to accommodate more foreigners and cope with the growing expansion of the city, which was also functional to the establishment of both the spiritual and temporal power of the Church in the period of the Counter-Reformation. Side effects, such as the opening of new roads, greater widespread wealth, and an increased interest in culture, favoured the arrival of many pilgrims from all over Europe who demanded adequate and efficient services.

Piazza di Spagna in different moments

Piazza di Spagna stood at the bottom of the hill known as the Colli degli Orti, leaning on the Pincio Hill that extended up to the Quirinale. The construction of the square, begun by Pope Clement VII, was continued by Pope Paul III Farnese after the Sack of Rome in 1527. In this period of religious turmoil, popes wanted the city to take on an image reflecting the new cultural and welcoming needs, making this place the heart of the city, sometimes even retracing northern European models. Thus, the Colli degli Orti, a luxurious terrace since imperial times, where the wealthy patricians had lived, was slowly being transformed into an elegant road to the port of Ripetta.

The church of the Santissima Trinità dei Monti, which towers above the steps, was also meant to be an ideal place for mystical praying solitude, far from the city humdrum but yet in the heart of Campo Marzio. It was conceived by a simple friar, San Francesco di Paola, who lived in the late 15th century and founded the convent for the Hermits Order. Still, by Pope Paul III Farnese's will, a connecting street was built between the convent and the river port, following the pipelines of the Acqua Vergine aqueduct, made in the imperial times by Agrippa, today Via Condotti. This project represented the birth of a new reality, functional to the great city repopulation. Over the centuries, the square was no longer just a passageway between the hills and the port but a place in itself, rich in trade, commerce, cafes and cultural venues, the sale of all kinds of objects and, not least, the site of art galleries, as described by travel writers and called "Platea Trinitatis." Because of its width, it was easier for many foreigners and artists to get there by carriage and they considered it to be the ideal place for Roman holidays in the centuries of the Gran Tour. During the two following centuries, the square, which had become an international icon, was also home to a variety of local characters such as villagers, florists, painters, writers, and merchants who gave life to a harmonious and elegant theatrical backdrop with the direction of the diplomatic representatives of France and Spain, who competed for the supremacy of the square. In the seventeenth and eighteenth centuries, the place experienced the peak of its glory, and both Bernini and Borromini collaborated in embellishing and arranging the grand palaces, once again rivals in their choice of patrons. Thus, the pope Urbano VIII Barberini, as a friend of the French nation, tipped the balance in the rivalry between the French and the Spanish. As a result, the construction of two palaces in the small space of Piazza Mignanelli was carried out, one commissioned by the pope in line with the French, Palazzo di Propaganda Fide, the other by the Spanish, who were building there the new headquarters of their embassy. Both the religious and the international spirit of the place were strongly emphasized. Confirming the friendship between the Pope and France, Pietro and

Gianlorenzo Bernini built the Fountain of Barcaccia, which celebrated the agreement between the two States. They decorated it with motifs of Barberini bees and the shining sun referring to the French king. They got the idea from a boat found there after the flood of 1598, which later became a symbol of the universal church sailing in stormy seas. It contains more than one meaning: the importance of the Church, the alliance with France, the glory of the Barberini, and the apotheosis of the Baroque.

The *Barcaccia*

To highlight the prevalence of France in the square planning, a large and monumental staircase was built leading to the French church located on top of the hill. The project took much longer than expected and was intended to stress the similarity between Alessandro Specchi's staircase on the port of Ripetta and the one on the hill by De Sanctis, an architect well-liked by the French. The design of the Trinità dei Monti staircase echoed Specchi's design and was adorned with the symbols of the different families. Several small streets connect the square to Via del Corso, fringed with buildings from the 1600s to the 1800s, and where time has conferred a kind of severe austerity, some times interrupted by shop windows. The whole area of Via del Corso can satisfy the taste of those who are fond of art, as well as of those who just like shopping. In any case, it is pleasant to stroll slowly along these small streets, admiring the fine decorations of a doorway or simply a beautiful view in the continuous *zigzagging* among the narrow alleys and then going back to Via del Corso. Among the many small streets that branch off from here is Via dei Greci, named after the *Collegium Graecorum*, where we find the church of St. Athanasius, designed by Giacomo della Porta, and at number 18, the entrance to the Conservatory of the famous Accademia di Santa Cecilia, a temple of classical music. The walk continues as far as Largo dei Lombardi, where we find the basilica of San Carlo al Corso, more exactly basilica of the Saints Ambrogio and Carlo, a church of the Lombards living in Rome and whose holder is the archbishop of Milan who celebrates service there in Norwegian three times of the year and by tradition the church becomes a meeting place for Norwegian "expats," including non-Catholics. Next, you get to largo Goldoni, so called because the famous playwright lived in the building at the corner with via Condotti, and where the elegance and luxury of a famous fashion house stands out. Here, fashion lovers can take a little side street on the left where they will find another temple of shopping by strolling down Via Condotti, from which there is an extraordinary view of Trinità dei Monti. In the springtime, the steps are richly decorated with azalea plants in bloom, set among the balconies of the side palaces, including the one that housed the famous English poet John Keats on one side and the elegant "Babington" tea room on the other. In the final part of Via Condotti, it is worth stopping at one of the oldest and most prestigious *cafés* in Rome, the *Caffè Greco*, dating back to the mid-1700s and which has had among its visitors important characters from the world of culture and even the future Pope Leo XIII.

R.Guttuso "Caffè Greco"

Other narrow streets run parallel to Via dei Condotti, and it is delightful to take a stroll there unhurriedly; these include Via della Croce, Via della Vite, Via delle Carrozze and Via Frattina, and many others, all ending up on Via del Corso. The staircase climbs up to Trinità dei Monti and invites to step up to discover its beauty, as well as the spectacular view of the city. We walk down Via Gregoriana to return to Via del Tritone, and we are fascinated by another gem of the Roman Baroque architecture of 1590: Palazzetto Zuccari. Its originality lies in the portal and the two side windows that are shaped like gaping jaws, recalling the park of the monsters of Bomarzo. The Palazzetto, now a renowned library, was a lively cultural centre attended by distinguished people and artists in the 19th century.

Palazzo *Zuccari*

Walking down to Via Capo le Case and Via della Mercede, you return to Via del Corso as far as Piazza San Lorenzo in Lucina, a bustling parlour. Next to fine stores, you can admire the basilica of San Lorenzo, which gives the square its name; it has very ancient origins, around the fourth century A.D., and has undergone later renovations. Its name comes from a Roman matron, on whose "domus" the present church was built under Pope Sixtus III; the first structure was completely rebuilt during the papacy of Pasquale II and completed in 1130.

Piazza San Lorenzo in Lucina

Further works were carried out in the 1600s, and the simple façade is evidence of the church's origin, not in line with the Baroque taste of the time but conforming to the Romanesque tower. Originally the interior had three naves, but the side ones were later converted into chapels, where numerous personalities have been buried, including the French painter Nicolas Poussin. One of the side chapels, belonging to the Fonseca family, was built by Bernini, and the main altar is a remarkable work by Carlo Rainaldi and contains a famous crucifix by Guido Reni. During recent excavations, the remains of a domus from the first century B.C. emerged in a room that had been home to the titulus *Lucinae*, while in other rooms are the remains *of the Horologium Augusti*, a large gigantic floor sundial, whose shaft was the obelisk standing now in Piazza Montecitorio. Piazza in Lucina is also the setting for noble palaces of great artistic value, thanks to the façades created by Valadier and later by Piacentini. Today it appears as an en *plain air* "salotto" animated by elegant cafes and fashionable stores.

Via di Campo Marzio, a nice shopping walk, winds from here, where designer shops invite to peek through shop windows, while imagination runs back in time to fancy about how this alley, so trendy today, might have been like in the past. Number 48 is a beautiful 18th-century palace adorned with decorations of female faces, a Moor's head and comet stars. It is remembered because it was the seat of Masonry, and further excavations in the area uncovered the remains of zodiac signs and a board with a series of perpendicular marks that refer to Augustus's sundial, whose map can be seen in the window of the annexed café. The small street is crowded with historical houses inhabited by illustrious personalities, and the one at number 2 is particularly rich in memories because Giuseppe Verdi lived there, as recalled by the plaque displayed: *"Giuseppe Verdi lived in this house in the winter of 1859 when the stages of Rome first heard the melodies of Ballo in Maschera while from the Alps to the two seas people's voices acclaimed his glory and in his name expressed the renewed hopes of Italy and pointed to the liberating King."* Not far away, a 16th-century house can barely be distinguished in the twinkling lights of the shop windows, but equally impressive is another building of the same three-story style, whose majestic portal is crowned by a harmonious balcony, supported by corbels where decorative heraldic elements in the shape of panthers stand out. Once you reach Via degli Uffici del Vicario, you can't resist the temptation of having an ice cream at "Giolitti's". While slowly tasting it, you will proceed to Via della Maddalena, where you will be on the edge of the important Pigna neighbourhood where the Pantheon is located. A short walk off Piazza in Lucina is also the delightful little square of Fontanella Borghese, overlooked by the majestic Palazzo Borghese, built in the second half of the 16th century to a design by Vignola and continued by Flaminio Ponzio on commission by Cardinal Scipione Caffarelli Borghese. The building was completed by Maderno and enlarged by Carlo Rainaldi. It is called the Borghese Cembalo because of its singular shape and is considered one of the four wonders of Rome, along with the Farnese's *Dado,* the Caetani's *Scala* and the Carboniani's *Portone.*

Palazzo Borghese

The inner arch-shaped courtyard surrounded by 96 granite columns is remarkable. Here, a fountain framed in the centre of the loggia arch stands out, and another is located on the opposite side; finally, a third one shows the wish to enrich the courtyard with abundant water. Mythological and pastoral themes are suggested by statues representing elements of Nature. The wing of the palace on the Tiber has a two-story façade that resembles the keyboard of a harpsichord. It is also known for its incomparable collection of paintings by famous artists such as Raphael, Domenichino, Caravaggio, Cavalier D'Arpino, and "The Madonnas" by Lorenzo Lotto, Andrea Del Sarto, and Giulio Romano, all of them are placed today in the Borghese Gallery, whose owner was still Cardinal Scipione Caffarelli Borghese. The palace is not open to the public, yet the glimpse we catch of the princely court through the majestic portal suddenly takes back to the splendour and glorious past of this opulent building. One of the most celebrated protagonists of this place was surely Pauline Bonaparte, Napoleon's beloved sister, who had married Camillo Borghese in 1803 and stayed here for a long time. Much has been fancied about her and her beauty when, barely 23 years old, she crossed the hall of this sumptuous palace and became its absolute lady. However, she immediately showed arrogance as she decided to close off access to one of the most beautiful and shady areas of the large Borghese garden, where people used to go to enjoy their free time. *"Pauline's personal suite, lit by the large windows on the fourth floor, to the right of the main entrance, still bears the imprint of her fastidious taste; it was specially decorated for her in the French Empire style. Many tales have been told of Pauline's way of life; the procession of lovers and the vanity that justified in her own mind her use of the ladies-in-waiting as footstools, also the curious habit of being carried to her bath, by a gigantic Negro. At balls, Pauline never condescended to dance but simply sat surrounded by her adorers"* (Giorgina Masson 1998). Even Canova, fascinated by her beauty, wanted to immortalize her in the famous statue of Venus Victrix, now on display at the Galleria Borghese, in which Pauline, challenging the morals of the time, poses showing her perfect forms. Though she was undoubtedly a frivolous and restless woman, she had all the makings of legends about her.

Following digressions into the past of the Borghese Palace, we continue our walk on Via della Scrofa, a narrow street that starts from Ara Pacis and runs to Sant'Eustachio neighbourhood. It was an important street in Roman times probably dating back to 29 B.C., and its name comes from a small stone bas-relief depicting a sow and used as the sign of an inn called "La Scrofa." One part of the imposing former Augustinian convent skirts the street, giving it a more important character.

Walking down Via della Pallacorda, we eventually get to Piazza Firenze, the heart of Campo Marzio neighbourhood and anciently the seat of institutional power, so much so that even today it is under the influence of the Chamber of Deputies and many politicians are daily seen swarming and crowding the narrow streets and local restaurants, just as the prefects once used to do. Its origin dates back to the sixteenth century and comes from the union of two patrician residences reunited into a single building that now houses the Dante Alighieri Society. The palace had undergone ups and downs over time, which were finally resolved favourably thanks to the intervention of the Duke of Florence, who became its owner and gave his name to the square. Indeed, piazza Firenze contributes to the cultural feeling of the place as a reminder of the crucial role that the city of Florence had played in the humanistic rebirth of Rome. Via dei Prefetti also talks about medieval history, dominated by the ancient lineage of the Prefetti di Vico, who managed to hold, in the name of the Pope, the position of "prefects of the city," an extremely important and prestigious task from 1297 to 1445.

Continuing along Via dei Prefetti, we return to Via del Corso to reach Piazza Venezia. The hustle and bustle mixed with the high-pitched clamour of the crowd gives the area an extreme dynamism, where it is easy to imagine the great figures of the past living there, their moment of glory and power. Walking past Palazzo Venezia and Piazzetta San Marco, leaving the Capitol on the left and stepping slightly into Rione Campitelli, we arrive at Via del Teatro Marcello, home to one of the city's oldest buildings, linked to the image of a great female figure. She was an extraordinary character whose actions crossed several neighbourhoods of ancient Rome, and her charitable work is evidenced by the many shelters she wanted to build to alleviate the pain of the poor and the sick. The figure of Saint Francesca Romana, who lived between 1300s and 1400s, went down in history as a woman of noble lineage, who had always rejected luxury in order to devote herself to caring for people in need. She was forced into marriage by her father when she was only 12 years old; she obeyed his wishes yet with great individual effort and suffering that also caused her illnesses. Her husband Lorenzo de' Ponziani, also a nobleman, was so much in love with her that he never wanted to force Francesca to abandon her vocation, even allowing her to found an order of lay nuns, the "Oblates," who followed the rule of putting themselves at the service of the deprived with untiring zeal. Francesca Romana began her religious formation in the area of Piazza Navona, then moved to the palace of the Ponziani family in Trastevere, where she lived with her husband. She was called "the poor girl of Trastevere", and during the 1402 severe famine, she opened the doors of her own palace, where wine, grain, oil and money were distributed to the poor, but she did even more, going to the nobles' homes to collect basic necessities. Stories about her miracles and healing have been told, which left the doctors of the time speechless. Her mission moved from Trastevere to the Monastery of the "Oblates" at Tor de' Specchi. Situated in the heart of Rome between Piazza Venezia, the Forums, the Capitol, and the Ara Coeli, its entrance opens onto via del teatro Marcello and has been the place of the Oblates for five centuries, who were neither bound by a real vow nor by enclosure. The monastery has managed to overcome attempts at confiscation while keeping intact its original charm, jealously guarded by the nuns. The place is open once a year, on March 9, Francesca's Day. Also, a mass has been celebrated here on Easter Thursdays for decades.

Its interior still contains the 15th-century courtyard with the manger of the little donkey that brought food, clothing and wood to the poor. The heart of the monastery is in the small chapel, a primitive hub of prayer, which houses a cycle of frescoes painted by Antoniazzo Romano and telling the story of Francesca's life and her prodigies, wrapped in a deep sense of Christian faith and bearing witness to the great work Francesca had done in the city. The oldest part of the complex is a staircase where there are remains of capitals and columns from the imperial era, taken from the Forums; the reception hall contains 17th-century tapestries painted with herbal colours and a monogram of Christ, JHS (Jesus Hominum Salvator) against the background of a sun, made by Bernardino of Siena. Upstairs, there is the nuns' dining hall, whose frescoed walls reproduce seventeenth- and eighteenth-century Rome, and finally the community chapel, with Bronzino's striking "Annunciation" in the centre, the monumental tabernacle with stones and the ancient organ, the choir and the wooden portal. A good part of the oblates' day was absorbed in prayers and meditations, and something curious to remember is that the first group of oblate women were from the Roman aristocracy, who were acquainted with luxury and were driven to the monastery by a genuine desire to practice the Gospel virtues and serve the poor. Men of faith had a foothold here, one of them was Don Bosco. Today only two oblates remain in the small, quiet and secluded world to testify their important charitable work.

Frescoes in "Tor dè Specchi Monastery"

Walking back down Via del Corso from Piazza Venezia, we enter the Colonna neighborhood, which owes its name to the Roman column of Marcus Aurelius dominating the square. It is 29.6 m. high, equal to one hundred Roman feet, and was commissioned by Commodus, successor and son of Emperor Marcus Aurelius. The scenes that adorn it, arranged in a spiral, evoke the military campaigns that the latter led on the northern borders of the Roman Empire against the Germanic tribes. The column has been damaged by earthquakes and has also undergone renovations that marked the passage of power from the Emperor to the Church and then to politics: the original bronze statue of Marcus Aurelius, placed at the top of the column, was eventually replaced by a statue of St. Paul, commissioned by Pope Sixtus V who strongly promoted the central role of the Church. Palazzo Chigi, the official seat of the Italian government, overlooks Piazza Colonna, it was built in the late 1500s by the Aldobrandini family and was purchased in the mid-1700s by Agostino Chigi. During this period, the palace was embellished with a splendid courtyard divided by Doric pillars, columns surmounted by arches and adorned with trophies of arms and crowns of oak branches framing a multi-pointed star. The decorative elements all recall the symbols contained in the coats of arms of the two families, Della Rovere and Chigi. The fountain placed in front of the entrance overlooking Via del Corso is also remarkable, showing a beautiful mask framed in a crown of oak branches. A few steps away from Piazza Colonna, it is possible to reach the neighbouring Piazza di Montecitorio, where the Chamber of Deputies of the Italian Republic is located; it is an impressive building designed by Gian Lorenzo Bernini and originally inhabited by the Ludovisi family. Large rooms enrich the interior, including the hall known as the "Transatlantic" for its vast size, which has become the centre of political life. A grand room leads to the Hall of Busts depicting deputies and presidents of the Chamber, as well as the Hall of Women, to commemorate the first women in Italian political history. Works of art and paintings of great value decorate the rooms.

Piazza Colonna

Palazzo Wedekind stands next to Palazzo Chigi, with a porch of Ionic columns of Etruscan origin, while an elegant fountain designed by Giacomo della Porta stands in the centre of the square near the column. Palazzo Ferrajoli, which marks the edge of the square, was built on the remains of ancient houses of the Roman nobility and has undergone various renovations since 1661, becoming the residence of high prelates, men of arms, and cardinals, until it returned to noble families in the mid-19th century. Entering the building from the main gate, you will find yourself in the courtyard that contains a beautiful fountain topped by the Ferrajoli coat of arms. An attractive female figure, reminding the goddess Minerva, stands with a mask casting water into a large circular basin, according to the Latin inscription *"both useful and ornamental"*.

In front of Piazza Colonna, on the opposite side of Via del Corso, the *Galleria*, named after the memory of the actor Alberto Sordi, is an elegant shopping arcade. Beneath the area, there used to be luxurious dwellings dating back to the imperial times, which formed almost an entire city with an annexed thermal area. Today is still possible to visit the remains of the ancient *"Portico of Vipsania"* carried out by the architect Agrippa and with the interesting rebuilding of what the whole site must have looked like originally. This is all located in the basement of the *Rinascente* store, where a comfortable room in front of the Roman remains allows you to relax and enjoy the images projected on the walls, recreating the original setting.

Images of the ancient ***Portico di Vipsania***

Continuing along Via del Corso, you will walk only a few meters to reach the prestigious Doria Pamphilj Gallery, a museum that houses very important works of art and is still owned by the homonymous family. As we walk down Via del Corso, we can enter a tangle of narrow streets and small squares by taking a side alley to the Doria Pamphilji palace, and all of a sudden, a Roman temple appears in all its majesty. We are in Piazza di Pietra, a small corner, overlooked by the columns of the Temple of Hadrian, which was erected in 145 A.D. by Emperor Antoninus Pius as a tribute to his foster father, Hadrian. The square probably owes its name to the piles of stone from the temple itself, which has been restored several times over the centuries. A monument of great value, it features 11 Corinthian columns and is one of the best-preserved architectural examples of imperial Rome. Around the 1600s, the lively presence of carriages made the narrow arcade host workshops for farriers, and the loopholes for the horses can still be seen. Since 1879 the structure has housed the Chamber of Commerce, the first example of how to make a historical building functional again in a modern context. The scenic effect that the colonnade offers to the square is impressive as it seems almost to shrink in front of such majesty and drag us into a distant age, where the world turned around the emperors' absolute will. Let us return to more recent times to tell something about Palazzo Ferrini Cini, built in the early 16th century. It is located near the colonnade and was built by a wealthy notary of the time; it was donated to the Augustinian nuns of Calvi, who entrusted its restoration to Ferdinando Fuga, an architect well known to the Apostolic Chamber, around the middle of the 18th century. Later, the palace was purchased by Count Cini.

Piazza di Pietra

Cloister in Sant'Andrea delle Fratte

Wishing to escape from the chaos of tourists crowding between the Trevi Fountain and Via del Tritone, it is worth taking refuge in a green corner hidden from the public view. It is the marvellous cloister attached to the Church of Sant'Andrea delle Fratte, a little paradise where master violin makers have found an ideal location next to the Music Conservatory.

Just opposite, on Via della Mercede, at number 11 and 12, are the two seventeenth-century buildings that had belonged to the Bernini family; in the former lived Gian Lorenzo, who had had his studio on the ground floor of that building until 1680. On the second floor are two lunettes commemorating important episodes in Bernini's life, including a visit to the artist by Pope Urban VIII. Later, the palace became the property of Assicurazioni Generali of Venice, as recalled by Saint Mark's lion. Another famous person who lived in the palace was the Scottish novelist Sir Walter Scott. The adjoining building shows a plaque with a bust of Gian Lorenzo Bernini that reads, "Here lived and died Gianlorenzo Bernini, Master of Art, to whom reverent popes, princes, peoples bowed." Though amazingly emotional, the inscription had been placed at the wrong house number because Bernini actually lived at number 11. Some street names and monuments here, such as Sant'Andrea delle Fratte and Via Capo le Case, suggest that until the 15th century, the area had been the edge of the inhabited land, beyond which the countryside began. At number 3 on Via Capo le Case, there is the peculiar building known as the "house of the puppets," because on the sides of the five windows on the second floor are placed striking caryatids. The writer Massimo D'Azeglio had lived and worked here for a short time.

"Casa dei Pupazzi" or Palazzo Toni

Nearby, there is Via dei due Macelli, so called because in ancient times, it housed two meat stores before the slaughterhouse was moved outside the walls. This street was a continuation of the ancient Via Paolina, now Via del Babuino, and at number 40 of Vicolo Due Macelli, you come across a very interesting doorway decorated with 24 stone loaf shapes, which suggested that the building was owned by a noble family that had originally been bakers.

Door with shapes of bread loaves

The modern via Sistina, originally called *Strada Felice* because it was wanted by Pope Sixtus V named Felice at the end of the 1500s, was characterized by an incredible length of about three kilometres connecting Trinità dei Monti to Santa Croce in Gerusalemme to facilitate the Jubilee pilgrims itinerary between the city major basilicas. Over the centuries, it was divided into several sections with different names: via Sistina, via delle Quattro Fontane, via Agostino De Pretis, via Carlo Alberto, via Conte Verde and via Santa Croce in Gerusalemme. Today, Via Sistina houses one of the city's most famous theatres, designed by the architect Marcello Piacentini and famous for Garinei and Giovannini's well-known variety shows. Thanks to the continuing success of its plays, it has been called by the American press "the Italian version of Broadway."

RIONI PIGNA AND SANT' EUSTACHIO

Located in the heart of central Rome, the small Pigna neighbourhood preserves some of the oldest monuments linked to the city history. You can't think of strolling through its narrow streets without considering the value and function of the various religious brotherhoods, first and foremost the Company of Jesus, wanted by St. Ignazio di Loyola. Born in the Basque Country in 1491 to a noble family, he had fought, distinguishing himself mainly for his military bravery until he was seriously wounded in the Battle of Pamplona. Forced to remain in bed, suspended between life and death, he had the chance to reflect on the value of existence for quite a long, and when he finally recovered, he converted to Catholicism. He wanted to travel to the Holy Land, where he became acquainted with the Franciscan friars and developed a deep religious faith. S. Ignazio wanted to deepen, study and spread it in every possible way. Back in Europe, he attended the Sorbonne in Paris, where he developed an even stronger faith, supported by firm dogmatic knowledge, convinced that the importance of education is the basis of any missionary work. He was an excellent communicator, able to entertain and attract people with his charisma. When S. Ignazio settled in Rome, he lived in the palace next to today's Church of Jesus, and there he decided to found the Jesuit order with the aim of fighting and defeating the heresies dominating the period. In 1534, he founded the *Compagnia di Gesù* and, soon afterwards, the *Roman College*, enlarged by Bartolomeo Ammannati, a Florentine architect. The building was regarded as the most important Jesuit school for all those who wanted to take the religious path, as missionaries in the world. There, the young men who arrived received a careful and detailed education in the Catholic dogmas and doctrines in a very strict context of observance of rules and precepts. Indeed, they had to be ready to face any kind of hardship and sacrifice, even to the point of accepting martyrdom to defend their faith. The two Jesuit churches in Rome were the Church of Jesus and the Church of St. Ignazio di Loyola. The former is located in the homonymous square dominated by Palazzo Altieri, which became famous in the 20th century because the actress Anna Magnani had lived there. Already known as "S. Maria della strada", the present Church of Jesus was financed by Alessandro Farnese in 1568 and built to a design by Giacomo Della Porta inspired by an idea of solemn austerity, fully in tune with the spirit of the Counter-Reformation. To be fair, it seems that the rich Spanish courtesan Isabella de Luna, who had counted Alessandro among her clients, had provided funds for the construction. The façade is entirely made of travertine, it has three entrances with Corinthian columns, numerous decorative elements such as coats of arms, half-columns, a double tympanum and a large window on top of which the monogram of the name of Jesus has been carved by B. Ammannati. The interior is simple, with a single nave, pointing directly to the altar, and all the Baroque decoration contributes to the strong effect of emotional involvement. Several popes belonging to noble houses the Ludovisi, the Barberini and the Pamphili have participated in the construction.

Chiesa del Gesù

In the middle of the church vault stands the "Triumph of Jesus Name ", a large fresco by the painter Baciccia (1679) with an extraordinary effect of perspective that seems to "exceed" the gilt-framed vault, supported by stucco angels. The great perspective invention creates the illusion of movement. The characters, swirling around the monogram "JHS" in heavenly light, seem to dance over the spectators as if flying in the great theatre of Faith, wrapped in the power of Jesus to fight against evil and heresy. On the left side is the chapel of St. Ignazio by Andrea Pozzo, with the niche covered with lapis lazuli and reliefs depicting the life of the saint, the statue of St. Ignazio and angels in silvered stucco by Pierre Legros. On the niche lies a large canvas by Andrea Pozzo, representing the saint receiving the red banner from Christ with the monogram of the *Jesus Brotherhood*. Through a Baroque device, the canvas is lowered so that the statue can be seen every day at 5:30 pm.

Among the most spectacular examples of Baroque in Rome is the Church of St. Ignazio, built by Pope Gregory XV in 1562 next to the Jesuit Roman College. The project, designed by various architects, including Carlo Maderno, shows a travertine façade, echoing the Church of Jesus with half-columns and pillars in two orders. The interior presents a single nave with three chapels on each side, in which there are works by Alessandro Algardi. The vault of the nave holds Andrea Pozzo's masterpiece of perspective illusion, portraying the glory of St. Ignazio. The saint is wrapped in a mystical light that comes directly from God and expands to all the members of the *Jesus Brotherhood*, who, with their apostolic mission, spread God's words to all continents, represented by symbolic images. Europe is painted as a queen on horseback, America as an Indigenous Indian woman, Africa in dark colour, and Asia riding a camel. In the centre stands St. Ignazio on a light-coloured cloud, and in front of him is the image of Christ slinging a cross. In the background we see other figures gradually fading away, creating a perspective depth. A ray hits the mirror with the symbol "JHS", reflecting the divine light toward the viewer. Another perspective game of high perfection can be appreciated by standing in the marble circle on the ground. Moving forward to the apse, the false dome, still painted by Andrea Pozzo with the trompe d'oeil technique, arouses great amazement because of its absolute sense of depth. Perspective deception is also evident in the four columns placed in the apse as they are situated on a concave surface, thus producing an idea of movement. On the chancel side is the Ludovisi Chapel with the funeral monument of Pope Gregory XV by Pierre Legros and four stucco statues representing the Virtues. Thus, the eye is seized by the light, colour and dynamic effect of the images created by the optical illusion.

Piazza Sant'Ignazio

Stepping out of the church, we find ourselves on St. Ignazio Square, a real stage where the placement of the three buildings circling the square makes an ideal backdrop for the theatre performances that used to take place there. The architect Raguzzini had, in fact, employed a concave design to welcome passers-by, the chromatic contrast between the white travertine on the church façade and the building's plaster hues make the overall effect even more striking. A short distance from the Church of St. Ignazio is Piazza della Rotonda, the centre of which is dominated by the Pantheon and features an elegant fountain designed by Giacomo della Porta. It is very popular because this is one of the most beautiful and iconic places in the city. Stendhal referred to the Pantheon as "the most beautiful remains of ancient Rome. A temple that has suffered so little that appears to us as the Romans must have seen it at the time." It was started by Marcus Vipsanius Agrippa,

Augustus's son-in-law and general, and in Roman times, it was rebuilt and enlarged; it is regarded as an architectural and engineering wonder of the ancient world, with its height equal to its diameter, and with a dome, still among the largest existing, that has overcome the pitfalls of time, so much so that it has served as a model for later centuries architects, because of the great care employed both in the choice of materials and distribution of weights. The distinctive feature of the dome is the *oculus*, a circular opening with a 9-meter diameter that forms the top of the dome and was designed to provide light and air inside the monument. The *oculus* is not completely open but is covered with a stone disk that protects it from rain and creates games of light and shadow, increasing the charm of the building. A remarkable feature is that when it rains, the interior does not flood thanks to two factors: an upstream current makes the rain droplets evaporate, while small holes in the floor drain the water, thus preventing the formation of puddles. Another eye-catching event is the shower of red rose petals thrown from the top of the *oculus* on Pentecost, a religious festivity that falls fifty days after Easter. The red petals commemorate the blood shed by martyrs to defend their religious beliefs.

Pantheon

Two important striking light effects occur inside the Pantheon, leaving the viewer amazed. On June 21st of each year, on the summer solstice, the sun's rays enter the oculus, projecting special light effects, in which the sun creates a huge luminous circle on the floor with a 9-meter diameter. Moreover, on April 21st, another extraordinary phenomenon occurs, whereby rays of light penetrate the Pantheon and, at twelve o'clock sharp, perfectly illuminate the bronze entrance door. In ancient Rome this was the day when the emperor entered the Pantheon totally enveloped by the dazzling beam of light. Afterwards, the temple became a Christian church, and today it houses the tombs of Italian kings, including Vittorio Emanuele II, as well as the burial of important artists such as that Raphael with an epitaph attributed to Pietro Bembo that reads, "Here lies Raphael, by whom nature feared to be vanquished while he was alive; but now that he is dead she fears to die." "*Monsignor Datario had fulfilled Raphael's wish that he wanted to go to the Rotonda. That church was a temple built by the Roman emperors. It was a majestic severity. One entered from the portico through eight very tall, old columns, and inside was a huge belly surmounted by a dome with an eye in the centre that gave light. It was the only church in Rome from which one could see the sky. Raphael had chosen to be buried there, under Paradise*" (from "Un amore di Raffaello" by Pierluigi Panza, Mondadori 2020). Near this famous temple is the Albergo del Sole, among the oldest in Rome, with its origins before 1500, and nearby in Piazza Sant'Eustachio, you can taste what is considered the best coffee in the city.

Going back to the crowded Pantheon Square, a few steps away, you will see the Basilica of *Santa Maria sopra Minerva*, an example of Gothic architecture. An elegant Egyptian obelisk with a little elephant at its base, designed by Gian Lorenzo Bernini, overlooks the little square. The church contains paintings by important artists and houses the tombs of numerous figures, including that of St. Catherine of Siena, patron saint of Italy, one of the famous Dominican friars known as Beato Angelico from the first half of the 15th century, and Bernini's funeral monument dedicated to the nun Maria Raggi.

Most impressive is Michelangelo's sculpture featuring Christ the Redeemer, in which the artist wanted to represent Jesus' full power after his resurrection.

Santa Maria sopra Minerva and the obelisk

In the convent next to the basilica, Galileo Galilei was forced to abjure his theses. The Catholic Church waited until the end of the last century to finally rehabilitate the father of modern science, erasing the condemnation that had been issued against him. *"I, Galileo Galilei..of my age of 70 years, personally constituted in judgment and kneeling before you Most Eminent and Most*

Reverend Cardinals...swear that always I have believed, believe and will believe for the future all that the Holy Catholic and Apostolic Church preaches and teaches. But because by this Holy Office...I have been judged vehemently suspected of heresy, that is, of having held and believed that the Sun is centre of the world and immobile and that the Earth is not center and that it moves, therefore I abjure, curse and detest the above errors and heresies...and I swear that for the future I will never again say or assert, in voice or in writing, such things for which one may have similar suspicion of me.." (Abjuration of Galileo Galilei, Rome Convent of Minerva, June 22, 1633)

Back again to the Pantheon, which you leave on your left, you will skirt Palazzo Madama, now the seat of the Senate, once owned by Margaret of Austria, the Emperor Charles V's daughter who had married Alessandro dè Medici, a nephew or perhaps the son of Pope Clement VII, in 1536. The marriage contract was meant to repair the breach between the Emperor and the Pope after the sack of Rome in 1527. Unfortunately, their married life lasted barely six months as Alexander was assassinated in an ambush and Margaret, known as "Madama", aged only 15, found herself a widow with a huge legacy to manage. Later on, she married Ottavio Farnese and lived permanently in the Medici Palace.

After a short walk we reach the church of San Luigi dei Francesi, temple of the French community in Rome, located in the homonymous square. Inside the church, there are numerous fine works, among which stand out the three beautiful canvases by Michelangelo Merisi da Caravaggio centred on the figure of St. Matthew and housed in the Contarelli chapel. The three works, characterised by the masterful use of light and dark ("chiaroscuro"), make the characters move as if on a stage, but at the same time in a natural and realistic way, achieving a perfect fusion of sacred and earthly life. Caravaggio emphasised real and human images, inspired by genuine compassion and strong intensity. The chapel dedicated to St. Louis, designed by Plautilla Bricci, the first woman architect in the early 17th century and who was also the author of the altarpiece that adorns the chapel itself, is also worth mentioning.

Those interested in Caravaggio will only need to walk a few more meters to reach the basilica of St. Augustine, after climbing a steep flight of steps. Inside, on the left, stands the "Madonna of the Pilgrims" by Caravaggio, representing the arrival of weary and exhausted pilgrims after a long journey to the Holy House, where the blessing of the Virgin Mary and Jesus relieves their efforts. In the foreground there is a poorly dressed man portrayed from behind with his bare, dirt-stained feet in evidence, symbolising obedience and devotion, key concepts of the *pauperistic current* to which the artist belonged. The poor and the humble have a prominent place in his paintings, in contrast with the opulent and lavish views of the Counter-Reformation Church, which Caravaggio challenged, considering himself a truer interpreter of Christian principles. The image of the Madonna appears particularly beautiful and sensual; in fact, the model Maddalena Antognetti, was known as a courtesan and painter's mistress. Caravaggio apparently donated this work to the church in exchange for the protection offered to him after he had injured a man who had heavily insulted his woman. According to the mentality of the time, that woman was certainly unsuitable to represent a sacred figure, but Caravaggio was evidently allowed more freedom because of the widely recognised artistic value of his works. Inside the basilica, you will also see Jacopo Sansovino's Madonna del Parto and Raphael's Isaiah the Prophet. Here was the sacred place where the first pews were reserved for the courtesans during services, away from the view of common people to avoid distraction. The tombs of many well-known female figures are found here, including the ones of Lorenzo Il Magnifico's daughter, Contessina dè Medici, and that of Fiammetta Michaelis famous courtesan in the city and lover to Cesare Borgia.

***Madonna dei Pellegrini* di Caravaggio**

It's easy to see how some churches in the centre of Rome are, in their own way, very small picture galleries, containing works of great and even exceptional artistic value.

Leaving the basilica, we walk down Corso Rinascimento as far as Corso Vittorio, where stands the imposing basilica of Sant'Andrea della Valle, which stretches into the Rione Sant'Eustachio. The basilica was built between the end of the 1500s and the beginning of the 1600s to the design of several important architects including Carlo Maderno. The interior evokes majesty, and numerous works of art can be admired. Fans of classical music will certainly know that one of the chapels was the setting for the first act of Giacomo Puccini's opera "Tosca." The church overlooks Corso Vittorio Emanuele II and is not far from Torre Argentina. The square was restored to its present form in the 1920s, it is dominated by the medieval *Torre del Papito* and the façade of the Teatro Argentina, dating from the early 1700s and still perhaps the most important theatre in Rome. The central part of the square is covered by an archaeological area belonging to Roman times, and it is said to be the place where Julius Caesar was assassinated during the conspiracy known as the Ides of March.

The Capitol, located a short distance from this square, is the smallest of the Seven Hills on which Rome was founded. It stands isolated and dominates the city from high, and since its origin, it has served its function as a fortress. From one rock called Rupe Tarpea, traitors condemned to death were thrown down. The square located on top of the Hill owes its final shape to Michelangelo, who also designed the monumental staircase, which is dominated by the medieval Palazzo Senatorio, currently the seat of the Rome City Council. In the centre of the square stands the statue of Marcus Aurelius on horseback, one of the most important

Roman emperors, whose figure is also recalled in the opening scenes of Ridley Scott's movie "The Gladiator". The present statue is a perfect copy of the original, completed in the 1990s of the last century, using the most advanced technologies, while the original one, made of bronze, is kept inside the Capitoline Museums to preserve it from erosion. These are considered the oldest public museum in the world, and there you can admire the "Capitoline She-wolf," the symbol of Rome; it is a bronze work by an unknown artist and perhaps placed in the fifth century B.C., although the dating remains uncertain. The twins placed under the she-wolf were added in the 15th century and are attributed to Antonio del Pollaiolo. A central palace that sumptuously dominates the square is adorned with a double-ramp staircase designed by Michelangelo, and beneath it, two large statues representing the rivers Nile and Tiber are located, whilst the one in the centre portrays Rome. An identical one depicting Minerva-Rome has been placed on top of the bell tower of medieval origin, known as the Patarina Tower. The palace stands on the site where there was originally the Tabularium and the ruins of the Temple of Veiove and has always been the place where senators met and, for this reason, called the Senatorial Palace. In ancient Rome a senator was a mayor as well and was elected to life among the patricians. Inside the Palace, there are many important rooms, including the Tapestry Room, the Hall of the Flags, the Hall of the Carroccio, and the Great Hall of Julius Caesar, adorned with his beautiful statue, where all the sessions of the Capitoline Assembly are held and where the flags of the 22 neighbourhoods of Rome are set. Finally, the Mayor's office placed on the Tower dominates the city. A spectacular view of the Roman Forum and the Palatine Hill, can be enjoyed from Capitol Square. Enthusiasts of antiquities will certainly be interested in walking through the Roman Forum, where there are numerous ruins worth noting; we wish to focus on the remains of the pedestal above which stood the "Golden Milliary" column where distances to the major cities of the Empire were engraved at the time when Rome was considered "caput mundi," the capital of the world. Santa Maria Antiqua, a church dating back to the 6th century, is also very interesting. Following an earthquake, it was completely covered by a landslide in the 9th century, only to be gradually brought to light again in the late 1800s and early 1900s. Inside, there is a cycle of frescoes dating back to the period when the church was built, and some of them are still well-preserved after more than a thousand years. In the distance, you can admire the massive shape of the Colosseum, perhaps the most famous monument remaining from ancient Rome, which has come down to our time in good condition.

"Here is an entity that has undergone so many drastic changes over the course of two thousand years, and yet it is still the same ground, the same hill, often even the same columns or wall, and in its people one can still find traces of its ancient character. Contemplating this, the observer becomes a contemporary of the great processes of destiny....." (J.W. Goethe Letters from Italy)

Turning your back to Palazzo Senatorio on the right, a steep flight of steps allows you to enter the Basilica of Santa Maria in Aracoeli. Its origin dates back to the 6th century and has come down to the present day after various extensions and renovations. The interior contains numerous tombs, including medieval ones, and works by important artists. The chapel dedicated to San Pasquale Baylon is worth a visit because it contains a beautiful fresco attributed to Pietro Cavallini, who worked between the late 1200s and the beginning of the following century. This painter, by whom few works have survived, is especially remarkable, as according to some scholars, he may have played an important role in the creation of the "St.Francesco's Stories " cycle located in the Superior Basilica of Assisi.

Moving away from the basilica, you can take the very long staircase leading to Piazza Venezia, which is dominated by the impressive monument to Vittorio Emanuele II, the first king of Italy and one of the Fathers of the Italian Risorgimento. This monument was begun in 1885 by Giuseppe Sacconi and modelled after Bramante's classical tradition, only to be completed about 50 years later. It was necessary to radically alter the urban balance of the area with the demolition of numerous houses. A large bronze equestrian statue dedicated to the king stands in the centre, and the curious will be amused to know that during an inspection of its interior, some plates and bottles were found which had probably been used when the workers celebrated the completion of the work with lunch inside the statue itself. The *Vittoriano*, which was erected as a monument to freedom and independence, is also usually referred to as the Patriots' Altar, especially since the body of the Unknown Soldier, a young man who died in World War I and never identified, was buried there in 1921; this tomb is located at the end of the grand staircase and is always guarded by a military picket. Roman people, who have always loved to mock the overly blatant displays of grandeur, ironically call the *Vittoriano* "the *typewriter*". Still, it is certainly interesting to wander around the monument's steps to admire the statues, sculptural groups, and all the works of art contained inside. Elevators on payment allow access to the top of it, where from the Terrace of the Quadrigae, you can enjoy a panoramic view of the city, with the Colosseum in the foreground. Such a scenic view also helps perceive the various important periods in the city history, sometimes even interrelated: the imperial Rome of the Forums, the Rome of the Popes with the dome of St. Peter's, and the Baroque Rome with the 17th-century palaces of Via del Corso. For those interested in military history, at the bottom of the Vittoriano is the entrance to the Shrine of Flags, a museum containing the flags of warships no longer in service and several military units.

On leaving the Vittoriano behind, you return to Piazza Venezia, where you can admire the Palazzo Venezia, which is imposing in size and was built around the middle of the 15th century. The Library of Art History and Archaeology is located inside. The palace was built in 1445 by the Venetian cardinal Pietro Barbo, who became Pope Paul II, and from then on, it was the site of many important historical events. A cheerful and convivial man, he lived in the mansion and loved leading a life full of fun and lively events. He was the one who introduced the celebration of Carnival in Rome, inspired by the Venetian tradition of the masquerades. It is said that he enjoyed watching the masked people to whom he would throw coins from the palace balcony. A well-known humanist of the time Mr. Platina, tutor to the Gonzaga family and a great expert in cooking, in his Roman stay, had described the carnival festivities as follows: "The old men ran, the young men ran, the Jews ran...the horses, mares, donkeys and buffaloes ran with much pleasure of all for the great laughter...Facing the window stood the Pope whose supreme taste and pleasure of these festivities took."

Next to Palazzo Venezia, St. Mark's Basilica is definitely worth a visit. Its interior contains Byzantine mosaics and other interesting works of art, including a 15th-century wooden ceiling.

Leaving the basilica, we return to Piazza Venezia where we can see the palace of Assicurazioni Generali, Italy's leading Insurance Company, which is very large and was also built in the early 1900s. Indeed, the entire square is dominated by huge buildings and a plaque on this building's wall recalls that Michelangelo Buonarroti had lived there. Unfortunately many old houses had to be demolished to raise new buildings in the area.

In every corner of a modern and somehow troubled city like Rome, history often meets art and offers cues for reflection, bits and curiosities that quickly carry you from the past to the present with sudden flashes as if you could still relive moments from other ages. We are almost jolted forwards and backwards as if in a slow-motion movie that drags time at its pleasure and makes it flow through our minds. It is even possible to hear the sound of horses pulling carriages amidst the hustle and bustle of hurried passers by, or find ourselves watching a Berber horse race rather than a spontaneous theatre show on a street corner or a crowded procession of pilgrims. These are instants of imagination that can even let you talk with Michelangelo or, stroll with Caravaggio or still attend a dance party hosted by Christina of Sweden.

It is the magic of this city.

BORGO

"We went to St Peter's Church, which the clear sky filled with a magnificent light, making every part of it bright and shiny. We were filled with the human enjoyment of that sumptuous and magnificent sight without letting ourselves be carried away by an over-sophisticated and pedantic taste, and refraining from harsh criticism. We enjoyed all that was to be enjoyed".

("Journey to Italy" by Johann W. von Goethe)

Borgo neighbourhood is very old and its name originates from 'Burg', quite an unusual name as it is of Germanic origin. It encloses a small centre, almost a fortress, which still retains the feeling of a village within a much larger centre, where everything turns around the life of St.Peter's Basilica. Even the little streets are not called streets, but "borghi". The complex was enclosed by high walls called Leonine, five kilometres long, built by Pope Leo IV between 848 and 852 after the attacks and sackings of the Saracens in order to protect the safety of the popes as well as the whole Vatican and prevent future invaders from intrusion.

Leonine Walls

Passetto di Borgo

From that moment, the settlement was considered a separate city, the "civitas leonina" with its own court and governors. Along the surrounding belt, equipped with rectangular towers, roofed in regular intervals, several gates were opened. Over the years, the walls were transformed and strengthened with the construction of new towers and continuous restoration of damaged parts together with the reinforcement of Castel Sant'Angelo have been regularly carried out. Since the 16th century, the threat of the Turkish invasion and the sacking of the city by the Lanzichenecchi have forced the popes to carry out new reconstructions for the defence of Rome, which were entrusted to Antonio da Sangallo. Numerous gates were inserted into the walls, in particular Porta San Pellegrino, Porta Pertusa, Porta Cavalleggeri, Porta Santo Spirito and Porta Sant'Angelo, all sentinels of the city which have witnessed real and widespread devastation as this vivid description of the Sack of Rome reminds:

"We walk in silence. From time to time we hear crackling and dull thudding, distant and close cries, the neighing of lonely horses, the barking of angry dogs, the yelping of exhaustion. The sound of footsteps is the only real thing that reveals our condition as survivors. Desperate not to scream, I murmur softly to myself, What a ruin! What a monstrous ruin! My God, there is nothing left alive; there is no one left!.... But if Rome, the first place of civilisation, had been ignominiously degraded, humanity itself was being degraded" (from "Rinascimento privato" Maria Bellonci).

Porta Sant'Angelo was one of the oldest entrances to Porta Leonina, dating back to the 9th century and bearing a long inscription by Pope Leo IV celebrating the construction of the walls:

"Romans, Franks, Pilgrims and all of you who admire this work, praise with a worthy hymn the good Pope Leo IV who has solemnly

consecrated it for the good of the Fatherland and the People. Together with the Supreme Prince Lotarius, who was happy and triumphant for many years, he provided the monument that celebrates his highest glory. A venerable faith tied them together with a knot of love; may Almighty God lead them to the Castle of Heaven. Its name is Leonine City."

Tiare Fountain at the Leonine Walls

In ancient times, this area was called "ager vaticanus" because it seems that "vaticinii" took place here and auspices were asked for the outcome of important battles or great undertakings. The area was rich in springs, such as San Damaso water and the Lancisian water. Originally, there were vineyards and cropped lands, perhaps dating back to Etruscan times. During the Augustan period, there were the gardens of Agrippina, Caligula's mother, who had a circus built here, later completed by Nero and called Circus of Caligula and Nero. The emperor Nero had his imperial villa built here, but it was destroyed in a fire.

One event, which took place in the first century A.D. and considered marginal by the then-despot of Rome, Nero, was actually what would radically change the importance of Rome in the spiritual life of the entire world. It was the violent mass execution of the first Christians, led by the preacher Peter from Palestine. The cruel, merciless massacre of a group of crucified people, mauled by hungry beasts or turned into living torches, was the occasion to gain favour with the crowds, who were crazy for bloody shows performed in the circuses.

During Christian time, the place became an important religious centre because it housed St. Peter's tomb, and it was there that Emperor Constantine, the first emperor to be converted to Christianity, built the first Vatican Basilica. Emperor Hadrian also had his mausoleum built in this area, which was transformed into a fortress and then into Castel Sant'Angelo, later used by Aurelian as a defensive stronghold. He also had the city walls built which were named after him. Unfortunately, however, the castle was not sufficient to limit the barbarian invasions.

This settlement, Borgo and its parts, was a sort of city annexed to the main one, and for many centuries the village had lived its own independent life, characterised by an international spirit. The whole of Europe ideally merged in this little extension of Rome, where crowds of pilgrims met thanks to Pope Boniface VIII's great invention, the Jubilee of 1300.

Lane in Borgo Pio

The citadel became the spiritual capital of Europe even during the period of the Crusades, the heresies, the Marine Republics and the spread of the Muslims. On top of Borgo was St Peter's Gate, the ideal entrance to 'paradise' for generations of believers from all over the world.

Borgo Pio, Borgo Vittorio and Borgo Angelico were the so-called new boroughs and, together with the old ones, formed the urban area that stretched as far as the Vatican City. All the boroughs had and still have the function of introducing to St Peter's Square.

S. Peter's Square with the Obelisk

Borgo has remained unchanged for centuries until the construction of the new St. Peter's Basilica and was annexed to the Reign of Italy with a popular referendum only after the proclamation of the Unity of Italy in 1861. One of the oldest buildings, founded in 727 A.D., was the Hospital Santo Spirito in Sassia, built to accommodate the Saxons who came to Rome on pilgrimage to St Peter's tomb. Hence, the German name "Burg" was given to this small area. In ancient times, the site hosted the Horti of Agrippina Maior, whose remains are still visible beneath the ancient building. It was considered one of the first hospitals in Europe and was built to provide shelter to pilgrims, poor people, the sick and abandoned infants, as evidenced by the Ruota degli Esposti (Baby Hatch) on the outside walls.

Hospital Santo Spirito in Sassia

Towards the end of the 12th century, Pope Innocent III entrusted the Knight Templar Guy of Montpellier with the management of the hospital. Pope Sixtus IV oversaw the restoration of the building after the fires and sackings, that had caused its degradation. In this period, the hospital was embellished with a cycle of frescoes narrating the pope's life and the story of the building, also known as the 'Sistine Ward". It is one of those buildings that are part of the series of precious historical constructions. We walk hastily, with our heads down, without ever looking up and everything around seems almost taken for granted. But if, while walking along Lungotevere in Sassia, we stop in front of its huge entrance, it is an easy step to push through the large gate leading into a rich court with an arched loggia. The interior contains important works such as an altar attributed to Andrea Palladio, a painting by Carlo Maratti and the portal by Andrea Bregno.

During the Renaissance, the palace was further enlarged and adorned with fountains and a beautiful quadrangular courtyard. There is an old apothecary shop, a place known as a pharmaceutical research laboratory, where the beneficial properties of many medical herbs were tested. On the same floor, the so-called *Salone del Commendatore* displays beautifully decorated frescoes telling the story of the hospital and the impressive Lancisian library is also located there.

The old apothecary shop

Back into the Borgo, a distinctive atmosphere pervades a tangle of narrow streets with fancy names, including Via dei Tre Pupazzi

(Three Puppets Street), named after a piece of marble on which three human figures are carved in the style of the 4th century, which must have belonged to one of the 'Via Triumphalis' rich sepulchres. Not far away, you will find Via degli Ombrellari, where generations of umbrella artisans used to live. In the middle of these narrow streets is the famous Piazza delle Vaschette, so called because it probably housed a fountain collecting 'l'acqua angelica' (angelic water), water that, thanks to its therapeutic properties, continued to attract people from various parts of Rome, who came with their flasks to take it. The silent square inspires a sense of profound peace and serenity and one cannot fail to notice a very old house, founded by Pius IX, which hosted Christian girls and in the past was the subject of a dispute between those who wanted to preserve it and those who wanted to destroy it. Fortunately, it remained standing, bearing witness to what Roman houses were like in the 15th and 16th centuries. Other alleys with imaginative names link the various borghi: Vicolo del Farinone, Vicolo del Falco, Vicolo del Campanile, with a beautiful Renaissance house with a graffiti-decorated façade, sadly known as the home belonged to Mastro Titta, the hangman of Rome, Vicolo d'Orfeo and Vicolo delle Palline, named after the six balls on the Medici coat of arms. It is worth mentioning a peculiarity of the Borgo's people, famous for being lively and hard-working, mainly made up of craftsmen with a strong patriotic streak. As evidence of this feature, there is a famous episode concerning the election of the new Pope after the death of Pope Gregory XI in 1378. The inhabitants of Borgo claimed that a foreign pope should not be elected and, shouting "We want him to be Roman", the Borgo leader summoned all the other boroughs and they all went to St. Peter's to make their request to the Sacred College. Thanks to their determination they succeeded in getting the point that the new pope would be Italian.

Walking along Borgo S. Spirito, the road climbs up towards Piazza S. Pietro which, thanks to the monumental grandeur of its two colonnades, welcomes the visitor as if to wrap him up in an atmosphere of sacredness and universality.

S. Peter's Colonnade

Due to its enclosed space defined by Bernini's magnificent colonnade, St. Peter's Square deserves more the name of Forum than that of square, thus recalling an ancient idea shared by both the Western and Eastern Roman churches. With its 284 columns and 88 pillars, the sequence of statues and the rhythms of the pilaster strips connecting the façade, the square seems to come towards the visitors and invite even the most indifferent ones to enter the temple of Christianity where they will be stunned by all the Catholic symbols triumphally displayed in lines, ornaments and colours. The columns, with Doric-style capitals, were designed to give the whole complex a heroic order suited to the figure of St Peter Martyr. The colonnade, built with the contribution of great architects such as Borromini, Peruzzi and Serlio, gives an illusion of maximum width so that one could easily imagine a sort of great theatre where events related to the Catholic faith took place, leaving life of the city out. The story of the square is very old, covering about 2000 years, and saw an initial transformation from Nero's circus in the imperial era into a cemetery until St. Peter's tomb was built after the Saint's martyrdom in the nearby Circus. It includes a very ancient red granite obelisk, about 25 metres high, coming from Egypt, from the city of Heliopolis and brought to Rome by Caligula. The bronze sphere on top seems to contain the ashes of King Salomon and of Julius Caesar. It is linked to a legend according to which Virgil, sent to Jerusalem by Augustus to find a suitable place for Caesar's ashes, found an ideal location in the ancient sphere. Using his magical powers, he managed to transport both the column and the globe to Rome in a single night. Two huge twin fountains, lined up with the obelisk and built by Maderno and Bernini, also adorn the square, transforming it into a more monumental place, benefiting from the new aqueduct that brought "Acqua Paola" to the entire Vatican area. A peculiarity of the perfect geometry of the colonnade can be seen by standing on one of the circular stones placed on the pavement; looking at the colonnade from there, the second order of columns disappears due to an optical effect and reappears as soon as you move out of the stone.

One of the twin fountains in S. Peter's Square

"At last, you come to Rome, the mother and queen of all things, which anyone who has not seen it, would be foolish to admire other cities. Just as the good fortune of Roman people made the city appear more beautiful, so the Jubilee Year will make it as spiritually beneficial as ever. The pilgrim will visit the Sepulchre of the Apostles; he will tread the ground that is red with the sacred blood of the martyrs; he will see the effigy of the Lord's face either preserved in the veil of the woman or present in the walls of the mother of all churches.... He will enter the Holy of Holies, a small place full of heavenly grace; he will visit the Vatican and the cemetery of Callistus, full of the bones of the blessed; he will see the crib of the Lord Saviour; he will contemplate the cut off head of John the Baptist, the grate of Lawrence; he will see where Peter was crucified and where after the shedding of Paul's blood, springs of

water sprang up; the place where, as a sign of the summer snow, the foundations of a beautiful temple were laid" (Familiar Epistles IX, 13 - Francesco Petrarch).

In the 4th century, the first Christian emperor, Constantine, wanted to build a basilica on this site to commemorate the Saint's martyrdom and celebrate the greatness of the new religious cult. Continuous changes were carried out by the various popes, including Nicholas V, who around the middle of the 15th century, transformed the beaten earth area in front of the basilica into a porticoed square, Pius II commissioned the construction of a marble staircase in front of the façade, and Alexander VI, on the occasion of the Jubilee of 1500, opened the first straight road, via Recta, between Ponte Sant'Angelo and the Vatican. This street, called Via Alessandrina and later Borgo Nuovo, created a very wide perspective in front of the great portal, in line with the papal wish to integrate the basilica into the complex that included the papal palace, the Curia and the residence. During the papacy of Julius II at the beginning of the 16th century, the pope decided to completely rebuild the basilica as part of a major urban requalification project.

The building site, popularly known as the "St.Peter's Factory", proceeded slowly and with a long list of architects that followed one another, such as: Rossellino, Bramante, Raphael, Antonio da Sangallo the Younger with Baldassarre Peruzzi, Michelangelo, Jacopo Barozzi da Vignola, Giacomo della Porta with Domenico Fontana and Maderno, Cavalier d'Arpino, Bernini and Pietro da Cortona.

After being totally overwhelmed by the whirl of the columns, you will suddenly feel that you are on the basilica's precious porch, where the polychrome marbles on the ground dazzle your eyes, and the majestic five doors invite you to enter this sacred place. Before crossing the main door, one cannot help but notice the two large equestrian statues of Carlo Magno by A. Cornacchini and Emperor Constantine by Bernini, the latter placed at the entrance to the Vatican buildings, which can be accessed via the Scala Regia. The atrium is adorned with 32 stuccoes representing various moments in the life of Peter, three inscriptions taken from the original Constantine church representing a donation of 56 olive groves, the epitaph of Hadrian I dedicated by Carlo Magno to the Pope and the Papal bill of Boniface VIII for the Jubilee of 1300. All the doors are massive; the one on the very left was made by Giacomo Manzù in 1964 and is known as the Door of Death because this is where the funeral processions of the popes leave. Four panels represent the Deposition of Christ, the symbols of the Eucharist, bread and wine, the theme of death as well as the death in exile of Gregory VII. Then comes the Door of Good and Evil by Luciano Minguzzi from 1970 to 1977. The Filarete door, or central door, was made under the papacy of Eugene IV in 1439 and has two bronze wings, each divided into three panels, illustrating Christ on the throne and the Madonna, St Peter and St Paul, the beheading of St Paul and the upside-down crucifixion of St Peter, framed by figures of animals with profiles of emperors. As a singular detail, it contains the artist's signature. The Door of the Sacraments, made by Venanzo Crocetti in 1965, features an angel announcing the seven sacraments. The one on the far right is the Holy Door, made by Vico Consorti and cast in bronze by the Marinelli artistic foundry in 1950 and donated to Pope Pius XII. In the 16 panels, you can see Pope Pius XII and the bill of Boniface VIII, who instituted the first Jubilee in 1300. It is opened exclusively on the occasion of the Jubilee.

The long and slow succession of changes and styles was progressive and evidence of the highest value celebrating the cult of the Catholic religion, which, from its initial uncertain beginning, was to assume a character of deep and spiritual universality over the centuries. The marvellous statues and paintings of Saints Peter and Paul, of the Virgin and Child, of the personifications of Virtue, of a "Pietà" capable of moving the hardest of hearts, all these seem to talk about grandeur and nobility.

Stepping through the doors of this monumental space, so enormous but at the same time so intimate and embracing, arouses strong emotions. Captured by the twirling of the statues that almost overlook the smaller world of men from high up. You are absorbed by the dynamism of the welcoming gestures of popes caught in the act of blessing crowds of devotees and angels that frame the scenes in an incessant dance of robes and garlands. The great architect of this sacred stage was Gianlorenzo Bernini, who became the faithful artistic executor of Pope Urban VIII Barberini, who was encouraging exceptional growth in arts and letters such as to be compared to the Medici splendour already started by Pope Leo X. The close relationship between the Pope and Bernini was almost perfect as never before in history, highlighting a complete correspondence of intentions between patron and artist.

In the early 17th century, Rome was experiencing a period of political, religious and military stability, so it became a sort of refuge for cultured foreigners to enjoy classical and contemporary beauty in a context of spiritual serenity. Bernini was the perfect interpreter of this desire, creating a majestic setting supported by the wealthy Barberini family. As early as the 16th century, Pope Julius II had strongly wanted to give the church a mark of beauty and grandeur in the world, and to do so, he had called upon the collaboration of supreme architects such as Bramante, Raphael, Antonio da Sangallo and then Michelangelo. It was a continuous alternation of projects in which ideas often overlapped, giving rise to controversy and changes, and the great architectural interventions seemed to be completed only in the seventeenth century when Carlo Maderno redesigned the façade, fulfilling a perfect synthesis between the proposals of Bramante and those of Michelangelo. In 1629, Bernini became the architect of St. Peter's for a long period of 50 years, when the basilica seemed to lose the simple and sober solemnity wanted by Bramante and Michelangelo to adopt a more decidedly baroque style. A complex decorative arrangement of columns, marble carvings, coloured medallions and white marble statues gave a chromatic vivacity and luminosity to the immense space. The refined Baroque scenery was enhanced by paintings, including mosaics by Calandra, cartoons by G. F. Romanelli and Andrea Sacchi and G. Lanfranco, and works by Pietro da Cortona, such as the "Trinity" painted for the Chapel of the Sacrament hidden behind Bernini's ciborium.

After the first moment of bewilderment at the vastness and richness of the works of art, once inside, you will be overwhelmed by the beauty of the chapel commissioned to Girolamo Muziano in 1578 and located under one of the smaller domes. The work is remembered for the introduction of a new mosaic technique, peculiar for its resistance and therefore also used for the dome decoration. Its creation is attributed to Cavalier d'Arpino, who produced the cycle of cartoons representing the sanctified Popes and Doctors of the Church, the Redeemer, the Virgin, St Paul, St John the Baptist and the Apostles; this is followed by three angelic circles, the most important of which represents instruments of the Passion. Everything ends with the dazzling brightness of the lantern where the figure of the eternal Father stands out. The chapel dedicated to Pope Aldobrandini was begun by Michelangelo and finished by Giacomo della Porta, and the mosaics were entrusted to Cristoforo Roncalli.

With Pope Urban VIII in the 17th century, greater emphasis was placed on the overall decorative richness assigned to Gianlorenzo Bernini, who created the bronze sepulchral canopy under the dome, which then became the main feature of the entire complex, with an absolute focus on the apse. The ceiling was the work of the young Borromini and was composed of dolphin-backed volutes. The columns are in line with the tradition of the ancient Constantine presbytery and were redesigned by Bernini in 1627 with a work on the baldachin where two rows of niches were created to contain the relics of four martyrs and their giant statues.

"In the nave, I was enchanted to admire the gigantic columns that the pope's sculptor, Gian Lorenzo Bernini had recently raised to the high altar by casting the bronze from the Pantheon vault. They twisted on themselves like candles, they didn't even seem to be made of metal, but of living matter. They were so gigantic that the space was transfigured." (From "L'architettrice" by Melania Mazzucco)

These were the impressions that the imposing canopy aroused, almost like a stage set ready for the sacred theatrical representation of Christian symbolism.

Bernini's Canopy in St.Peter's

Bernini was also the creator of two burial monuments dedicated to Urban VIII and Alexander VII, which are not simply decorative but deeply symbolic. The one for Urban VIII shows the Pope in the act of blessing the crowd and is made of very dark metal. The personifications of Justice and Charity represent the virtues that survive the Pope's life in the collective memory.

The monument dedicated to Alexander VII shows the figure of the Pope kneeling, surrounded by Charity, Truth, Prudence and Justice, all wrapped in a large cloak under which Death can be glimpsed holding the hourglass of time.

Alessandro VII's burial monument by Bernini

These funerary works inspired another great architect, Alessandro Algardi, who created the pyramid-shaped tomb of Leo XI in 1644, again representing the blessing Pope, a copy of which decorates the wall of the staircase leading to the Vallicelliana Library. Funerary chapels dedicated to the great popes succeed one another, hosting statues of saints and martyrs, alternating with frescoes and oil paintings containing stories from the Old Testament. There are also mosaics such as the Martyrdom of St. Sebastian painted by Domenichino, and mosaics by Pietro da Cortona, also author of the beautiful altarpiece portraying the "Trinity." The nave is at the centre of this row of chapels, an immense space 90 metres long and 26 metres wide, covering an area of approximately 2,500 square metres and topped by a large barrel vault, culminating in the monumental cathedra behind the St Peter's canopy . The design of the marble floor is highly refined, containing ancient parts from the former Constantine Basilica, such as the large red Egyptian porphyry disk. It has become a symbol of power since Carlo Magno knelt down there on his coronation on 25th December 800 by Pope Leo III, as well as other emperors such as Frederick Barbarossa and Frederick II of Svevia.

Red porphyry disk

The marble floor was created by Gianlorenzo Bernini on 1650 Jubilee year, together with the decorations of the nave. The interior surfaces are covered with about 10 thousand square metres of mosaics by many great artists such as Pietro da Cortona, Giovanni De Vecchi, Cavalier d'Arpino and Francesco Trevisani. The niches in the pillars contain numerous statues of saints, including the ancient bronze statue of St.Peter by Arnolfo di Cambio. The holy fonts are about two metres high and were made between 1722 and 1725.

Moving towards the right aisle, into the first chapel is situated the famous "Pietà" by Michelangelo, completed in 1499 that expresses a perfect synthesis of harmony, purity and mysticism, arousing a strong empathy with the human tragedy that is portrayed.

La Pietà by Michelangelo

"The Pieta is intended to be an exemplarily Christian work of art, the theme of desire is contrasted and opposed to the complementary theme of regret, expressed through an anxious vibration of the soul. The Madonna holds the dead Christ on her lap as if he were a sleeping child, and she looks just as young as when Christ was a child. The statue may be a vision, or rather a prediction or foreshadowing of the passion of the Virgin's son. The prediction is immediately linked to regret; the demonstrative gesture of her hand says that the prediction has unfortunately come true..... The composition is closed as if in a pyramid, to indicate that everything is part of a divine design, which transcends human pain and piety" (Giulio Carlo Argan Storia dell'Arte Italiana-Il Rinascimento).

The composition recalls a spiritual theme dearest to Michelangelo that the artist could develop as a member of the Circle of the Spirituals, where he met the poetess Vittoria Colonna. From their deep friendship, characterised by a great spiritual affinity, emerged rhymes, letters and drawings, evidence of a mental evolution that would encourage a renewal of the Catholic Church and a return to a purer spirituality freed from the growing system of corruption. In a previous drawing dedicated to Vittoria, Michelangelo reinterprets the feeling of piety according to the tendencies introduced by the Protestant Reformation, showing the Madonna in the background compared to the centrality of Christ and underlining the great themes of passion and salvation. Here pain, compassion, gratitude and beatification are the great themes highlighted by her look and her arms turned to the sky in a gesture of human despair. The same ideas are expressed in Vittoria Colonna's spiritual rhymes, where the element of Pietà overcomes despair and mourning, through the hope of Resurrection and the triumph of life over death.

To Vittoria Colonna:

"A man in a woman, or rather a God, speaks through her mouth, whereby I am so much absorbed in listening to her, that I shall no longer be mine. I firmly believe, since I was taken away from her, that I should have pity for myself; so much so that her beautiful face spurs me on, that I see death in every other beauty. O woman who passes through waters and fire the souls of my days, deh, make me no longer return to myself" (Rime, Michelangelo).

While digressions wander free, inspired by such a beauty, the carousel of sculptures continues to show itself in all its perfection. We stop in front of the monument by Carlo Fontana dedicated to Cristina of Sweden, the "Martyrdom of San Sebastiano" realised on a drawing by Domenichino and the monument by Canova elegantly inlaid on a precious pink marble for the Stuarts. Particularly noteworthy in the ambulatory is a mosaic reproduction of Raphael's famous "Transfiguration".

If inside the basilica astonishes for its size and its dazzling collection of works of art, outside "The Dome" is the symbol of the whole city as well as of the whole Christianity, the destination of pilgrimages from the remotest places in the world. Evidence of this is widely testified in the reconstructions of *Scholae Peregrinorum* and other charitable institutions that arose in the Middle Ages around Peter's Sepulcher. Its majesty bewilders because it stands out in the sky like a protective shield that, though never suggests an idea of defense, rather gives a sense of peace and universality gathering the entire Christian world around immortal values such as justice, brotherhood and virtues, placing itself almost halfway between the earthly world. and the spiritual one.

Monument to the Stuarts by Canova

The "Dome" from Borgo

Inspired by an idea of perfection, already expressed in the Pantheon and in Brunelleschi's dome in Florence, using the circle as the shape of such perfection, it was finally realised by Giacomo Della Porta in only two years from 1558 to 1561, after an intense planning work made by Michelangelo. Getting up to the top of the dome is an experience worth doing if you are ready to climb 551 steps and overcome increasingly narrow spaces that eventually turn into tunnels with a strong slope. The exhausting climb to the top of the dome, through the long and winding staircase, also known as St. Andrew's snail, offers a first stop on the side balcony that overlooks the interior of the basilica. From here you can experience new and intense emotions, admire all the masterpieces from a different and more exciting perspective and discover those small details that can only be perceived at close range. The last stretch of the climb, which is more and more challenging, rewards the effort with a unique view of the entire city. Monuments, streets, palaces, bridges, the Tiber with its bends and the many churches with their soaring domes crowding the squares and streets, draw a gigantic tapestry of vivid and harmonious colours as if to evoke a magnificent work of art. Up there, from that dizzying height, the so-called *sanpietrini* (men working at the Basilica) showed off their great acrobatic ability to move confidently on the dome, gliding quickly from one side to the other on the winding, narrow stairs to fix various pieces of equipment, exhibiting unsuspected talents, inventiveness and technical skills. The team composed of masons, electricians, and carpenters, led by Nicola Zabaglia (1664), was praised for carrying out extremely valuable works, whose devices have survived time.

In the 18th century, an extraordinary light exhibition was offered to visitors on St. Peter and St. Paul festivities, when the dome was enlightened with countless torches and lanterns placed around the dome walls by *sanpietrin*i workers suspended on ropes and cables. *"The dome seemed to catch fire, almost as if it wanted to extinguish the star light in the sky,"* as Goethe had commented.

The dome was built over a period of many years under Michelangelo's direction and started in 1554 with the supply of travertine from the quarries of Fiano Romano, and work was completed after 1561 when the last internal and external capitals were completed. The dome, seen from the inside, rises up to the junction between the nave and the transept. The external tambour is formed by a base on which sixteen round buttresses with rectangular windows are set. Giacomo della Porta worked very fast and planned the covering of the external dome with lead plates. During the same period, the smaller domes around the main one were made, and finally the interior decorations, mainly in mosaic, were carried out on designs by Cavalier d'Arpino and Giovanni de Vecchi. The structure was also reinforced and curved by Giacomo della Porta and Domenico Fontana, who inserted a series of chains into the walls to resist the cross thrusts exerted by the vault, and they hinged the travertine slabs with molten lead, which prevented the dome from being damaged in the 1703 earthquake. On top of the dome stands a sphere surmounted by a cross. This bronze ball plated in gold was accessible to visitors until the mid-20th century. It is said that Pius IX was the last pope to go up there in 1847 on St. Peter's Eve, whereas Pope Gregory XVI hosted a reception for the Zar Nicholas I in 1845. The splendour and worldliness of the popes, ambassadors, cardinals and the entire papal curia are also expressed through the great complex of the Vatican Palace, which is located within Vatican City. The world's smallest State, simply called the "Vatican," founded in 1929 by the Lateran Pacts, is an enclave within the Italian Republic headed by the Pope. The small State has its own life, issues its own stamps, has its own newspaper

'L'Osservatore Romano' and its own radio station. It had already been annexed to the Italian Reign in 1870 and has been reduced in size to the present area surrounding St. Peter's Basilica. Inside there are the Apostolic Palace, the Governor's Palace, the Vatican Gardens and the Vatican Museums, which deserve special mention for being one of the largest art collections in the world. Founded by Pope Julius II in the 16th century, they contain works such as the Sistine Chapel and the papal flats frescoed by Michelangelo and Raphael, as well as a picture gallery with works by Giotto, Leonardo, Raphael and Caravaggio. In the more modern section, there are paintings by Carlo Carrà, Marc Chagall, Salvador Dalì, Giorgio De Chirico, Venanzo Crocetti, Paul Gaugin, Vassilij Kandinskij, Henry Matisse and Vincent Van Gogh. There are also Greek-Roman sculptures, donations from all over the world, an Egyptian museum, an Etruscan museum, works of Roman art, ancient stone inscriptions, collections of tapestries and maps. The climax of beauty and mysticism is achieved when you finally reach the sacred place of the Sistine Chapel, an icon of the entire and complex theological representation. "*Without viewing the Sistine Chapel, it is impossible to shape an appreciable idea of what one man alone is capable of accomplishing*" (J.W.Von Goethe).

Here the first signatures of this masterpiece were left by Perugino, who began the decoration of the wall behind the altar, and Pier Matteo D'Amelia, who created the vault with the starry sky. Thanks to Lorenzo de Medici's contribution, great artists such as Sandro Botticelli, Cosimo Rosselli and Domenico Ghirlandaio were sent to Rome. In collaboration with Pinturicchio, Pietro di Cosimo and Bartolomeo Della Gatta frescoed the panels on the right wall of the altar, which were also enriched by Luca Signorelli, who painted the Moses Testament. The result of this extraordinary joint effort was a spectacular cycle of figures and scenes taken from the stories of the Bible in which details, gold trim, and suggestive lighting effects enhanced by a constant rhythm stand out. In the XVI century Giulio II della Rovere decided to restore the vault damaged by a crack, entrusting Michelangelo Buonarroti to carry out the works. He worked from 1508 to 1512, facing many obstacles and therefore being forced to build by himself a simple scaffolding placed on supports stuck in the walls. It was a terraced scaffolding so as to facilitate the work on the entire surface to be decorated. Michelangelo should have painted only the twelve figures of the Apostles, but he actually completed more than three hundred of them. Over the years several structural renovations were carried out to repair the damaged parts as well as to satisfy the pope's wish to show off their prestige through overloaded decorations. The last great work was ordered by Clement VII, who charged Michelangelo with the huge fresco known as "The Universal Judgement", painted on a surface of about 160 square meters between 1536 and 1541. Through the complexity and richness of the work, the artist represented a moment of crisis in the great Renaissance values that had placed man at the centre of the universe, endowing him with almost absolute powers. He seemed to revise this optimistic view by presenting an image of mankind forced to face its own weaknesses and inabilities and, therefore, submit to the divine judgment.

"No painter has ever done anything like this, and never was there a more horrible sight. They are the wretched condemned dragged to the torment by demons. Michelangelo translated into painting the frightful images that Savonarola's fiery eloquence had once impressed on his soul. He chose an example for each of the deadly sins... One of the damned seems to be trying to escape. Two demons drag him into hell, and he is tormented by a huge serpent; he is holding his own head in his hands. This is the truest image of human

despair. Our 19th century most advanced civilisation would give us an uglier picture of despair by showing it in a human being who lacks everything, even his vital force. It is usually through the figure of this damned that travelers begin to understand the Last Judgment. There is not even the slightest idea of this either among the Greeks or the moderns." (From Stendhal's Roman Walks, 1828).

This fresco aroused some polemics by Cardinal Carafa, who had accused Michelangelo of excessive realism, almost touching indecency because of the nudity of some figures. Being such an impressive work made in the temple of Christianity, it could not avoid negative criticisms but also gain praises, such as Vasari's comments in his "Lives" who described it as follows: *"Besides any extraordinary beauty..., so properly painted and conducted,.... and in the true multitude of figures, the terribleness and greatness of this work is such, that you can not describe, being so filled with all possible human affections and having all beautifully expressed."* Like many other critics, Vasari had seen perfection in Michelangelo's portrayal of the human body's infinite motions. The central theme of the fresco tells the story of the Last Judgement, when a man stands before God to undergo the judgment that will accompany him in his afterlife. The artist worked intensely and passionately on the work and its colour combination and was so totally involved in the process that he did not want any help and did not allow anyone else to participate. This commitment caused a sudden fall from the scaffolding, which kept him away from work for about a month.

Leaving the museums, you may feel puzzled by a whirl of thoughts and wonder how man may have generated so much beauty with his genius, creativity and passion to get even beyond the perfection of Nature. Past the monumental granite obelisk in St. Peter's square, coming from ancient Egypt and decorated with papal coats of arms, you will pass through the lion's gates and be back in the borgo again. Otherwise, following an ancient secret passage called the "Passetto di borgo", you might walk eight hundred metres along a narrow elevated walkway running in the walls connecting the Vatican with Sant'Angelo Castle. The Passetto was built to allow the Pope to flee quickly and unseen to Sant'Angelo Castle in case of enemy attacks. It was built in 1277 by Pope Nicholas III and allowed Pope Alexander VI to take refuge in the Castle in 1494 during the invasion of Rome by the army of Charles VIII of France. In 1527, Pope Clement VII also used this passageway during the Sack of Rome by Charles V's Lanzichenecchi. Going through this secret passage, it is easy to imagine the frantic running of the popes in danger, followed by the crowded throng of bishops and cardinals who wanted to escape capture or a merciless end. The castle, which was a defensive fortress of Rome, saved the Vatican from being plundered by the Visigoths and Vandals in the first half of the 15th century, but its history is much older, dating back to 135 A.D. when Emperor Hadrian had his own funeral mausoleum built on this site, inspired by Augustus' tomb.

Sant'Angelo Castle

The complex consisted of a marble-clad cubic base with a frieze decorated with ox heads, where the names of the emperors buried there could be read. A peperino and cement tambour, covered with travertine, stood above the cube. On top of this was a tree-lined earthen mound surrounded by statues, and among them, the best preserved is the Fauno Barberini, an ancient Greek sculpture from the Hellenistic period representing a sleeping satyr. Inside the mausoleum, in the urn chamber, you will be enchanted by the verses that make up the epitaph pronounced by Emperor Hadrian (138 A.D.) on his deathbed and placed on his tombstone: "*Little soul, lost and gentle, companion and guest of the body, now you are preparing to ascend into colourless, harsh and bare places, where you will no longer have the usual games*".

A wall with a bronze gate decorated with gilded bronze peacocks ran all around the mausoleum. It housed Emperor Hadrian and his wife, Emperor Antoninus Pius and his family, Emperor Marcus Aurelius and his sons, Emperor Septimius Severus and his family, and Emperors Geta and Caracalla. In 403 A.D., the building lost its function as a sepulchre and became a fortress to defend the city against foreign invasions. In 590, Pope Gregory I organised a solemn penitential procession to support the city hit by a severe plague. As the pope was crossing Ponte Elio, today Ponte Sant'Angelo, he saw the archangel Michael on top of Hadrian's mole, sheathing his sword, which was considered a heavenly sign predicting the end of the plague.

Sant'Angelo Bridge

The two defensive towers and its strategic position close to St Peter's made the castle a highly desirable residence, the object of dispute among the city's various powerful dynasties such as the Crescenzi, Pierleoni and Orsini families, but in the late Middle Ages, the building was handed over to the Pope, so that it could officially become the Vatican stronghold. In the centuries that followed, the Popes took care of its embellishment and restoration, making it more and more efficient. During the Sack of Rome, it became a permanent papal residence, so much so that the decorations in the pope's personal apartments were enriched, while the main role of the entire complex remained that of a fortress and a prison. The castle cells were used to imprison the pope's opponents, such as Benvenuto Cellini, whose cell still displays a charcoal drawing of a resurrected Christ on the wall. The Count of Cagliostro, a Freemason, magician, alchemist and healer who used to devote himself to practices opposed by the Church, was imprisoned in a luxurious cell for noble prisoners. Among the famous people were Giordano Bruno and Beatrice Cenci, whose death sentence was carried out in the square just in front of the castle. Later, in the 19th century, the castle was used for different purposes as barracks and as the seat of the Military Engineering Museum. Giacomo Puccini set his opera Tosca here in the last century, and a group of famous designers such as the Fontana sisters, Emilio Schuberth and many others organised important fashion events. In 1954, Luchino Visconti filmed some scenes of the movie "Senso", and it has also been the setting for several Dan Brown novels.

As you leave the castle, you feel as if you had walked through 2000 years and relived moments of glory as well as moments of terror, where the prevailing feeling is still the original need to defend the territory and the spiritual values pervading it. In front of the large square facing the castle is the Sant'Angelo bridge, formerly Elio bridge, built by Emperor Hadrian in 134 A.D. and so-called after the emperor's second name. It joined the two banks of the Tiber, connecting the two important neighbourhoods of Borgo and Ponte. Sadly known in the past for being a place of executions and exhibitions of corpses. In 1500, it was embellished with the statues of St. Peter and St. Paul, and during the visit of Charles V of Spain in 1536, it was further enriched with eight stucco statues representing the Evangelists. The restoration of the bridge in the 1600s brought about the construction of stone balustrades and iron gates, and the ten angels by Gian Lorenzo Bernini, with the symbols of passion, replaced the ruined stucco statues.

Under the watchful and amused gaze of the statues set high above, multitudes of pilgrims from all over the world, crowds of busy merchants, hasty bishops and cardinals have always crossed the small bridge in a continuous back-and-forth to discover the sacred places that bear witness to universal Christianity.

BIBLIOGRAPHY

- “Rinascimento Privato” Maria Bellonci 1986
- “Il giornale di viaggio in Italia” Michel E.Montaigne Edizioni Paoline 1963
- “L’architettrice” Melania Mazzucco, Einaudi 2019
- “ La vita quotidiana a Roma ai tempi di Gian Lorenzo Bernini” Almo Paita 2021
- “Nuove Isole” Marco Lodoli, Einaudi 2014
- “I cieli bellissimi” Giovanna Giaume, Merlino Edizioni
- “Roma che nessuno conosce” Claudio Colaiacomo, Newton &Compton Editori,2021
- “Storia sociale dell’arte” Arnold Hauser, Einaudi 1955
- “Antichi mestieri di Roma” Mario La Stella, Newton &Compton Editori, 1982
- “Piene storiche del Tevere a Roma” M. Bencivenga e P. Bersani 2001
- “Vicende e monumenti di Roma” Tina Squadrilli, Staderini Editore 1976
- “Lucrezia Borgia” Maria Bellonci, Oscar Mondadori 2019
- “I rioni di Roma” Silvio Maurano, I e II vol.Casa Editrice Ceschina, 1964

- "I rioni di Roma" di Giuseppe Baracconi, Edizioni Colosseum,1986
- "I vicoli di Roma" Giorgio Carpaneto , , Newton &Compton Editori Editori 2005
- "Feste e ricorrenze tradizionali romane" a cura di Francesco Rutelli, Tascabili Economici Newton,1998
- "Lettere" Percy Bysshe Shelley, Cinquemarzo edizioni, 2016
- "La Roma di Bernini" Federico Gizzi , Newton &Compton Editori 1996
- " Veni, vidi.vici" Peter Jones, Atlantic Books London 2013
- "Scopri Roma, i vicoli" M. Richter, P. Morandi, Polo Books 20008
- "I Ponti di Roma" Giuliano Malizia, New Compton edizioni 1995
- "Le Sette Chiese" Paolo Coen, New Compton editori 1994
- "Itinerari romani" ,Viator, Franco Spinosi Editore, 1966
- "Storia dell'arte italiana" Giulio Carlo Argan , Sansoni , 2006
- "I cortili di Roma" Ludovico Pratesi, New Compton editori 1994
- "Le Cupole di Roma" Ludovico Pratesi, New Compton editori 1995
- "Passeggiate Romane" Stendhal, Feltrinelli 2019
- "Rione Regola" Ludovico Pratesi, Ludovico Pratesi, New Compton editori 1997

- “Roma e i Romani “ Aristide Gabelli, Il Parnaso, 2000
- “Il memoriale di Paolo dello Mastro” di Stefano Infessura, Treccani.
- “Le piazze di Roma Capitale” di Armando Ravaglioli), , New Compton editori 1995
- “Piazzette di Roma” di Armando Ravaglioli, Tascabili Economici Newton.1995
- “I palazzi dei principi romani” ” di Armando Ravaglioli, New Compton Editori 1996
- “L’Emigrante” di Ljubov Dostoevskaja 1912
- “Le grandi piazze di Roma” di Armando Ravaglioli, New Compton Editori 1996
- “I palazzi del potere” di Armando Ravaglioli, New Compton Editori 1996
- “Il Tevere” di Armando Ravaglioli, New Compton Editori 1995
- “Gabriele D’annunzio: Roma fine Ottocento” a cura di Paola Sorge, New Compton Editori 1995
- “Il Rione Borgo” di Ludovico Pratesi, New Compton Editore 1998
- “Il Rione Ponte” di Ludovico Pratesi, New compton editore 1997
- “Geografia” Libro X di Strabone di Amasea,Edizioni dal Sud,2020
- “Le Epistole “ di Francesco Petrarca

- "Le Vite " di Giorgio Vasari
- "I segreti di Roma " di Corrado Augias, Mondadori,2006
- "The Companion Guide to Rome " di Giorgina Masson, Companion Guides,1998
- "Roma Sparita" negli acquarelli di Ettore Roesler Franz, di Livio Jannattoni, New Compton Editori,2013
- "La signora delle Fiandre" di Giulia Alberico, Piemme,2021
- "Storie e luoghi segreti di Roma" di Cecilia Gatto Trocchi, Newton &Compton Editori,2005
- "La storia di Roma in 501 domande e risposte" di Fabrizio Falconi, Newton Compton Editori,2020
- "Letters from Italy" by J.W. Von Goethe, Penguin Books
- "Viaggio in Italia " di J.W. Von Goethe Oscar Mondadori, 2013
- "The portrait of a lady" by Henry James, Penguin Books Ltd,2011
- "Roman Walks" Stendhal,1828
- "Storia dell'Arte Italiana-Il Rinascimento di Giulio Carlo Argan, Sansoni Editori
- "Abjuration of Galileo Galilei, Rome Convent of Minerva, June 22nd, 1633
- "Un amore di Raffaello" by Pierluigi Panza, Mondadori 2020

- "L'onore perduto di Isabella dè Medici" by Elisabetta Mori, Garzanti 2011
- "Rome. The inner light of a glance" by Gina De Bellis,Palombi Editori, 2017

Made in the USA
Las Vegas, NV
11 May 2025

21877469R00108